HOW TO END

A LOVE STORY

The Breakup Guide to Let Go, Level Up, and Never Settle Again

by

TESSA MONROE

How to End a Love Story : The Breakup
Guide to Let Go, Level Up, and Never
Settle Again

TABLE OF CONTENTS

INTRODUCTION

Ending a romantic relationship is rarely easy. Despite how often heartbreak touches lives, its ache feels uniquely personal, an internal storm that shakes the foundations of your very sense of self. Whether the parting is sudden or long anticipated, it leaves a profound void that few experiences can match. This book is designed for those moments right after the final goodbye, when clarity seems distant and emotions run wild.

Facing the end of a love story demands courage. It's a journey through pain, confusion, and deep reflection—sometimes all at once. Many find themselves wondering, "How do I move on without losing who I am?" or "Can I heal without forgetting the good parts?" These questions are on many minds, and the answers are never simple, but they are attainable.

One of the first things to understand is that heartbreak isn't just about sadness or anger. At its core, it's a disruption of the life and identity you've built with someone else. The dreams you shared, the daily routines you took for granted, the hopes for your future together—all of these get upended. Navigating this upheaval isn't just a matter of "letting go"; it involves carefully untangling your emotional threads and reconstructing your sense of normal.

Healing is not linear, and recovery isn't a race. Each person's path unfolds differently, shaped by individual histories, personalities, and the unique nature of their relationships. For some, healing may feel slow and painstaking. For others, it might be swift and cathartic. Either way, the goal remains the same: to come through heartbreak with a sense of clarity, strength, and renewed purpose.

You might feel overwhelmed by a flood of emotions, from grief and regret to relief and hope. It's natural to wish for quick fixes or simple answers, but the process often requires sitting with discomfort and leaning into vulnerability. This willingness to face tough feelings head-on is what ultimately leads to growth. It's in acknowledging the pain and honoring the experience that healing begins to take root.

This book offers guidance that balances empathy with practical wisdom. It's built on insights gathered from experts in psychology, personal growth, and emotional resilience, but most importantly, it reflects a deep respect for the complexity of human connection. The goal is to empower you—not just to survive a breakup, but to thrive after it.

Within these pages, you'll find tools to help you cultivate closure and peace. Closure isn't about returning to what was or shutting down thoughts about the past; it's about making peace with the reality of what happened and reclaiming your narrative. This newfound clarity allows you to step into the future unburdened by the shadows of old wounds.

It's important to embrace the fact that ending a relationship creates space—space to rediscover yourself and nurture new dreams. Sometimes it can feel like you're losing your footing, but this unsettled time also holds the possibility for profound transformation. You have the chance to rewrite your story in ways that honor your worth and align with your deepest values.

When you're struggling, it's easy to feel isolated or misunderstood. This book recognizes that and fosters a sense of solidarity. You're far from alone in confronting heartbreak's challenges. Many have walked this path before, finding healing and growth. Their journeys illuminate the way forward, showing that it's possible to rise from the ashes with resilience and grace.

Ending a relationship can also teach invaluable lessons about self-trust, boundaries, and emotional intelligence. These are not just tools for recovery; they're skills for living a fuller, more authentic life. As you work through this process, you'll begin to see your strength in new light—a strength that is born not from avoiding pain, but from meeting it courageously.

Whether this breakup is your first or one of many, the emotional terrain can feel daunting. It's a deeply human experience marked by intense highs and lows. This book approaches that reality with compassion and respect, offering strategies that are both heart-centered and actionable. You'll be encouraged to engage with your feelings honestly, build healthier boundaries, and create ripples of positive change in your life.

Beyond healing, this journey is about reclaiming your sense of self and opening the door to new possibilities. You may find yourself exploring parts of who you are that faded during your relationship or discovering passions that were sidelined. This process isn't just about finding closure but about renewing your connection to yourself and the world.

Breakups also challenge the stories we tell ourselves about love, worth, and happiness. Through this book, you'll be invited to rewrite those narratives, leaving behind limiting beliefs and welcoming a more empowered perspective. This new outlook helps prevent repeating old patterns and supports healthier choices moving forward.

At times, the road ahead might feel uncertain or lonely. That's natural. Healing doesn't mean forgetting love or negating the importance of the past; it means integrating all parts of your experience so you can move forward as a whole person. Each chapter will build on this foundation, guiding you with tools and insights to navigate the stages of recovery.

The end of a romantic chapter isn't just about loss—it's also about the promise of renewal. It's the moment when you step into your own power and decide what comes next on your terms. This book aims to be your companion as you transform heartbreak into a catalyst for growth, self-discovery, and lasting happiness.

In these pages, you'll find carefully crafted advice, emotional support, and actionable steps designed to help you heal with grace. Together we'll explore how to grieve fully, establish healthy boundaries, rebuild your identity, and eventually open yourself to joy and connection once more.

This introduction is just the beginning. What follows is a comprehensive roadmap for navigating one of life's toughest transitions. Whether you're seeking comfort, clarity, or motivation, this guide will help you emerge from heartbreak not just intact, but stronger and more self-aware.

Your journey toward healing and empowerment starts here. The chapters ahead are windows into what's possible when you approach the end of a relationship with honesty, compassion, and hope. You don't have to carry the weight of heartache alone—there's a way forward, and it leads to a brighter, more resilient you.

CHAPTER 1

---◇---

THE BREAKUP
BREAKDOWN

When a relationship ends, the flood of emotions can feel overwhelmingly chaotic—like your world has been rearranged without warning. That moment it truly ends often sneaks up quietly or explodes suddenly, leaving in its wake confusion, denial, and a whirlwind of hope that things might still change. This emotional rollercoaster isn't just in your head; it's wired deeply into your brain's chemistry, creating real physical pain that can be just as intense as any injury. Understanding why it hurts so much is the first step to reclaiming control over your feelings, giving you the clarity to set healthy boundaries and resist the urge to reach out impulsively. Instead, embracing the power of firm decisions and self-respect lays the groundwork for peace, helping you navigate the initial rawness and begin to envision a path toward healing and renewal.

The Moment It Ends

That instant when you realize a chapter has closed isn't just a fleeting feeling—it's a seismic shift that shakes up everything you thought you knew about love and yourself. It's messy and raw, often filled with a jumble of relief, sadness, and disbelief all at once. But this moment, as painful as it is, serves as your breaking point and your breakthrough. It's where clarity begins to pierce through the fog of confusion and denial, giving you permission to accept the truth instead of clinging to what once was. Embracing this moment with honesty and courage lays the groundwork for real healing, empowering you to move forward with intention, rather than getting trapped in cycle after cycle of what-ifs. Ending a love story isn't about erasing the past—it's about honoring what was, learning from it, and choosing the strength to rewrite what comes next.

Signs It's Truly Over When a relationship ends, one of the hardest questions to face is whether it's actually done—whether the closing scene you just witnessed is the real finale or merely a temporary intermission. In this moment of finality, it's crucial to recognize the signs that confirm the story between you and your partner has genuinely reached its conclusion. These signs aren't always loud or dramatic; often, they're subtle shifts in feelings and dynamics that accumulate until there's no room left for sustaining the connection. Understanding these indicators helps you embrace the truth with clarity and without holding on to false hope that only delays your healing.

One of the most telling signs that it's truly over is the erosion of hope in what the future might look like together. Hope isn't just wishful thinking; it's the emotional fuel that keeps people reaching for "what could be." When you notice that you no longer hold onto that hope, or that hope fades consistently after revisiting your expectations and dreams, it's a meaningful indicator. The hopeful visions you once had no longer hold emotional weight, and even your imagination gravitates toward separate paths rather than shared ones. This doesn't happen overnight but rather as a slow unfolding, often accompanied by a sense of emotional exhaustion when thinking about the relationship's potential revival.

In addition, communication—or rather, the lack of meaningful communication—is a profound sign. When conversations drift toward surface-level exchanges or dissolve into tension, it signals a broken bridge. You might find that attempts to discuss feelings or resolve conflict feel futile or repeatedly escalate into frustration on both ends. More than that, there is a shrinking space for vulnerability, where walls go up instead of openness. This disconnection isn't merely a bad phase; it reflects a deeper withdrawal of emotional availability that makes true reconciliation increasingly unlikely.

Trust, the bedrock of any intimate relationship, also responds to the finality of a breakup. The absence or deep fracture of trust means the foundation can no longer support the structure of what you once had. When trust is gone, even small actions or words trigger defense mechanisms that isolate rather than connect. You may notice a prevailing skepticism when hearing your partner's explanations or promises, a disbelief that colors every interaction. Recognizing that trust cannot be rebuilt overnight—and sometimes not at all—is part of acknowledging the definitive end.

Another key sign comes from how conflict feels. In a sustained relationship, disagreements can lead to growth and understanding, even if it's difficult at times. But once the relationship has truly ended, conflicts start to feel cyclical and irresolvable. You find yourselves stuck on the same arguments that produce more pain than progress. There's no longer a sense of partnership working toward a solution but a pattern of hitting dead ends. If this repetitive loop leaves you feeling drained rather than motivated to mend, you're likely facing a turning point where closure is the healthiest next step.

Feelings themselves often morph during this realization phase. Instead of the warm, complex mix that a lasting relationship nurtures, emotions grow colder or more indifferent. You might feel a growing emotional distance, an absence of excitement or curiosity about your partner's day or inner world. This emotional numbness or apathy isn't about malice or bitterness but signals a natural shutdown to protect your heart. It's the mind's way of signaling that the investment of care is waning because the connection no longer feels viable or safe to maintain.

Comfort also tells a story at the end of a relationship. Early on, you might have found joy in your partner's presence even during quiet moments. But as things wind down, there might be an internal resistance to shared silences, or awkwardness where ease once lived. Being around your partner might feel more exhausting than rejuvenating, as if you're operating on autopilot without the emotional nourishment you used to get. When the relationship becomes a source of stress or anxiety rather than solace, it's a strong indicator that the emotional contract between you has been broken.

It's important to pay attention to your own ability to envision a life without this person in it. If the idea now stings less than before, or maybe even offers relief, that's a clear sign the relationship's end is sitting more comfortably in your heart than the idea of continuing it. This shift is powerful; it represents an internal acceptance and readiness to proceed independently. It suggests you are moving toward reclaiming your agency, which is crucial for rebuilding your identity outside of the partnership.

Sometimes, signs show up in the way you respond to your partner's absence. Instead of yearning or obsessing over lost moments, your mind starts to wander freely, preoccupied by other interests, ambitions, or relationships. This natural realignment of focus away from the breakup signals emotional detachment—a process that enables healing. Accepting this evolving attention is an essential step toward embracing either closure or a fresh start.

Another subtle but vital sign is the diminishing influence your partner has over your emotions and decisions. When you no longer find yourself asking "What would they think?" or "How would they feel?" before making choices, a fundamental shift has taken place. This might feel like reclaiming personal power and independence, a positive move toward a healthier future. It also acknowledges that your emotional ecosystem has started to function without them as a critical input, which is necessary for growth after loss.

Physical cues can't be ignored either. The energy you expend around your partner might start to sap rather than invigorate. Instead of feeling a spark or warmth, you could notice a heaviness or fatigue that washes over you when interacting. Your body, which often knows the truth before your mind does, might signal the accumulated tension of unresolved conflict or mismatched needs. Becoming attuned to these signals enhances your understanding of the relationship's state.

On the flip side, you may find yourself seeking distance deliberately or unintentionally. This might be through avoiding plans, cancelling meetings, or finding reasons not to engage. It's not about rejection or hostility but rather a protective mechanism allowing space to breathe and think. When this pattern becomes consistent and longing for proximity diminishes, it supports the realization that the emotional and relational connection has faded.

When reflecting on all these elements together, it becomes clear that "It's truly over" does not rest on a single event or conversation but on a constellation of emotional shifts, behaviors, and realizations. It's a composite truth that you arrive at when your heart, mind, and body agree that continuing is no longer healthy for either person. Knowing this empowers you to close the door decisively and compassionately, allowing you to channel your energy toward healing and renewal.

Finally, recognizing these signs grants permission to yourself to mourn fully and move forward without guilt or confusion. It removes the gray area that drags out pain and keeps you stuck in cycles of denial or wishful thinking. Accepting the end as real frees you to rebuild with intention and strength, nurturing a vision for the future that honors your worth and the lessons learned from what was.

Denial, Hope, and Emotional Whiplash is that wild collision of feelings that rolls through you just after the relationship ends. It's the chaotic in-between space where your mind refuses to fully accept the breakup, even as your heart desperately clings to the possibility that this pain might somehow be temporary. When the moment it ends finally arrives, the emotional rollercoaster hasn't slowed down—instead, it picks up speed, twisting you between denial, hope, and overwhelming confusion.

At first, denial creeps in like a defense mechanism. It whispers that this can't be happening, that the breakup is some kind of mistake or misunderstanding. You might find yourself replaying conversations, searching for signs that it's not really over, or hoping that your ex will call back and say things were just blown out of proportion. This phase isn't just about avoiding the reality—it's your brain trying to shield you from immediate shock. It's a kind of emotional buffering, a way to keep the pain at bay just long enough for your heart to prepare. But denial, while protective in the short term, can also trap you in an unproductive loop where acceptance can't begin.

Hope often sneaks in beside denial as if they're dance partners in this messy breakup tango. Sometimes, it's the spark you need to keep moving forward. Other times, it becomes a slippery slope, fooling you into imagining reunions or impossible scenarios that delay healing. That hope might look like telling yourself, "Maybe they'll realize what they lost," or "Maybe we just need some time apart." These thoughts are natural— they come from wanting to believe in a future where love remains. However, clinging too tightly to hope without acknowledging the breakup's reality can cause emotional whiplash. You swing between moments of optimism and despair, never fully rooted in either.

Emotional whiplash itself feels like being caught in a relentless tug-of-war between conflicting feelings—and it's exhausting. One minute, you wake up feeling ready to rebuild your life; the next, you're hit with a wave of sorrow so intense it knocks the breath out of you. Your mood, your thoughts, even your energy fluctuate wildly from hope to heartbreak, from anger to numbness, from clarity to confusion. It's like your emotional compass spins out of control and you're left trying to find north in a storm where every direction feels wrong.

This whiplash isn't just a side effect of pain, it's a natural response to the loss of both a partner and a future you'd envisioned. The brain struggles to make sense of the sudden absence—why this had to end, where things went wrong, and if there's any way to fix it. Psychologically, you're negotiating the loss of attachment while still emotionally tethered to what was. It spawns inner conflict that feels deeply confusing and overwhelming, as your heart and mind battle over what to believe and how to feel.

It's important to recognize that this phase doesn't mean you're weak or failing in any way. The wild range of emotions reflects your mind and body trying to make peace with a seismic shift. While denial and hope can keep you stuck, they also hint at your deep human need for connection and meaning. We want to believe the people we loved will come back or that the break was just a bad dream. That's understandable—and even brave, because hope is a doorway, after all, not a trap unless you let it become one.

What separates growth from stagnation here is how you hold onto hope and deny reality. A healthy approach is to acknowledge your feelings without judgment, allow denial its space briefly, but gently guide yourself toward acceptance. It's okay to want to believe in the good, yet it's crucial to pair that with clear-eyed honesty about what is and isn't possible. Balance means feeling the sadness and confusion fully, giving yourself permission to grieve, but also reminding yourself that healing begins when you stop chasing a story that's over.

One of the reasons this emotional phase feels so intense is because endings lay bare that the person and the life you co-created aren't coming back as you knew them. You might still picture anniversaries, conversations, inside jokes. These memories can feel like a cruel double-edged sword, offering comfort and crushing loss simultaneously. This push-pull dynamic keeps your heart tethered and prolongs the twisted hope-denial cycle. It's like trying to hold onto water; the tighter you grip, the more it slips through your fingers.

During the moment the breakup hits, every interaction, text, or memory has oversized meaning.

A simple glance or message from your ex can trigger that emotional jerk—flipping your sense of progress in an instant. You might catch yourself blaming, pleading mentally, or bargaining for a different outcome, each cycle creating fresh pain but also stirring up a flicker of hope that "maybe this time" things will change. These wild swings often catch people off guard because hearts don't work like logic. They're messy, irrational, and fiercely loyal—even when loyalty is misplaced.

Part of navigating this chaos involves understanding that emotional whiplash isn't a flaw; it's a sign you're deeply human and capable of feeling great love. The intensity of these feelings marks the depth of your connection. Yet, to regain control, you'll need to start disentangling your feelings from your future. Hope can help you imagine new possibilities, but it shouldn't chain you to what was.

No matter how painful, facing the moment of "it's truly over" is where transformation begins. It's in owning both your hope and your denial without letting either dominate that you start to reclaim your power. Emotional whiplash slowly steadies as you learn to hold your feelings with compassion while also setting firm boundaries for your healing. Gradually, that momentum lets you move through grief rather than stuck in it.

Practically, this means creating moments of stillness where you examine your feelings honestly without rushing to fix or suppress them. It's perfectly normal to feel uncertain and conflicted—accept those feelings instead of pushing them away. Journaling your thoughts, speaking with trusted friends, and acknowledging your pain aloud can help bring clarity. Naming these conflicting emotions reduces their power and reminds you that this is a process, not a state you're doomed to remain in forever.

Hope isn't the enemy; it's the way forward when balanced with self-awareness. When you begin to notice patterns in your emotional swings—when hope strays into denial or denial locks down your capacity to heal—you can pause and gently course-correct. Remind yourself that the goal isn't to extinguish hope but to grow a stronger, more grounded version of it: one that supports your healing journey rather than obstructs it.

By appreciating the complexity of denial, hope, and emotional whiplash after a breakup, you normalize the messy feelings that flood your heart. You give voice to the confusion and hold space for the contradictions inside you. Most importantly, you start the crucial work of embracing your grief with courage and patience, opening the door to healing and eventually, to a future that feels full again.

Why It Hurts So Bad

Breakups cut deep because they're not just about losing a person—they shake the foundations of your identity, your future, and the sense of security you built around someone else. When a relationship ends, your brain responds almost as if you've experienced physical pain, triggering real heartbreak symptoms that make moving on feel unbearably difficult. It's the collision of emotional attachment, shattered hope, and the rewiring of neural pathways that keeps you stuck in that painful loop. Understanding this pain isn't about dwelling on suffering—it's about recognizing that your feelings are valid and part of the healing process, which lays the groundwork for eventually reclaiming your strength and clarity. The hurt feels overwhelming because it's a sign that your heart was truly invested, and that's the first step toward rising stronger on the other side.

The Neuroscience Behind Heartbreak Pain Exploring why a breakup can feel as devastating as physical pain takes us into the intricate workings of the brain. When a relationship ends, the ache isn't only emotional; it's biological. Our brains register heartbreak much like they would an injury, activating neural pathways that overlap with those responsible for physical pain. This is why phrases like "my heart hurts" or "it feels like a punch in the gut" resonate so deeply—they're not just metaphors but reflections of actual brain processes.

Studies using brain imaging reveal that the same regions that light up during episodes of physical pain—particularly the anterior cingulate cortex and the insular cortex—also activate in response to social rejection. These areas are crucial in processing distress, making heartbreak a uniquely painful experience on a neurological level. The brain doesn't distinguish between a broken heart and a bruised body as sharply as we might think. They are experienced together in a very real, tangible way.

Understanding this neural overlap is crucial because it debunks the myth that heartbreak is just "all in your head" or something you should simply "get over." It roots the pain in something deeply biological, emphasizing that your suffering is valid. You're dealing not only with lost love but with a neurochemical storm that makes moving on feel so challenging. This knowledge can nurture compassion for yourself rather than frustration or self-blame.

One of the key players in this neurochemical upheaval is dopamine, often known as the brain's "reward chemical." During a relationship, dopamine surges when you're around your partner or even thinking of them, rewarding your brain with feelings of pleasure and attachment. When the relationship abruptly ends, that dopamine supply drops sharply, triggering withdrawal symptoms remarkably similar to those experienced with substance addiction. This biochemical crash is part of why heartbreak feels compulsive—why many people find themselves obsessively replaying memories or reaching out when they know they shouldn't.

Oxytocin and vasopressin, often dubbed "bonding hormones," also play a significant role. These chemicals help cement emotional connections, fostering feelings of trust, security, and attachment. When the relationship dissolves, the sudden absence of these hormones contributes to feelings of loneliness and emotional distress. It's no wonder breaking up can feel like a void opening where once there was closeness and safety.

The brain's plasticity—its ability to adapt and rewire—gives us hope despite the intensity of this pain. Over time, repeated exposure to loving, secure interactions, and intentional healing practices can recondition these neural pathways. But at the moment of heartbreak, the brain is effectively hijacked by circuits geared toward survival and alarm, signaling danger at the loss of a significant attachment. Evolutionarily, this makes sense. Being part of a social group was critical to survival, so losing that connection would raise a red flag in the brain's threat detection system.

Another dimension to consider is how the amygdala—our brain's alarm center—reacts during a breakup. It heightens emotional responses, especially anxiety and fear, fueling the overwhelming rush of emotions that can feel unbearable. This hyper-vigilance to social threats magnifies heartbreak pain, often causing many to relive rejection moments repeatedly, stirring fresh waves of distress.

What this tells us is that the pain of heartbreak isn't just a fleeting emotional blip but a fundamental, physically grounded experience. When you feel that crushing sadness, anxiety, or emptiness, your brain is actively processing loss, rejection, and attachment pain as if your very survival is at stake. This explains why healing takes time and why patience with yourself is essential during the rawest phases of grief.

Interestingly, the insula, involved in both pain perception and emotional awareness, also lights up, giving heartbreak a visceral quality. You might literally feel the pain in your chest or stomach. This physiological response blurs the lines between body and mind, underscoring that heartbreak is a full-body event, not just an emotional one. Our bodies react alongside our emotions, reinforcing why self-care that attends to physical health—like movement, nutrition, and rest—can support emotional healing.

Neuroscience also sheds light on why people sometimes engage in behaviors that might seem counterintuitive post-breakup, like repeatedly checking a partner's social media or holding onto mementos. These actions are part of the brain's efforts to resolve uncertainty and regain a sense of control, attempting to soothe the cortisol-driven stress response. Although these behaviors might temporarily ease anxiety, they often prolong the pain by keeping neural pathways associated with the former partner overly active.

Recognizing the neurobiological underpinnings can empower you to approach heartbreak not just with emotional courage but with practical strategies that respect how your brain works. For instance, understanding the dopamine withdrawal cycle helps explain why it's completely normal to feel restless or irritable and why replacing old patterns with new, healthy routines is a critical part of recovery. Deliberate activities that stimulate positive neurotransmitters— like exercise, creative pursuits, or social engagement— can gently recalibrate your brain's chemistry.

At its core, heartbreak is a powerful example of how love and loss are deeply rooted in our biology. It's proof of how connections transform our brain's architecture, shaping not only who we are but how we experience the world. Accepting this truth can foster self-compassion and patience, reinforcing that the pain you feel is part of a complex, natural process designed to help you ultimately heal and grow.

The neuroscience behind heartbreak pain challenges the notion of simply "moving on quickly" or "getting over it." It highlights why grace, time, and structured healing approaches work best. As you navigate the aftermath of a split, keep in mind that your brain is essentially rewiring, relearning how to find pleasure, security, and identity outside of that lost connection. With time, intentionality, and kindness toward yourself, those neural circuits will shift, and the ache will lessen.

Because heartbreak isn't just a chapter in your story; it's a biological experience that demands respect. What feels like unbearable pain is the brain's way of signaling change, growth, and the necessity for new connections—starting first from within yourself. Holding this understanding close can become a steady anchor amid the storm, reminding you that healing is not only possible but inevitable.

Understanding Emotional Attachments is essential when diving into the heart of why breakups can feel like an emotional earthquake ripping through your world. When a romantic relationship ends, it's not just about losing a partner or a shared future; it's about untangling deep, often invisible threads that bind us emotionally to someone else. These attachments form the core of why letting go feels so agonizing—even when we know the breakup is for the best.

At their core, emotional attachments are the bonds we develop through consistent closeness, affection, and mutual support. They provide us with a sense of safety and comfort, much like the way infants rely on caregivers to meet all their emotional needs. Over time, these early processes evolve, but the fundamental craving remains: humans are wired to connect and to feel secure within those connections. When we lose that sense of security because of a breakup, the brain interprets it as a form of loss that threatens our survival. It's one reason why the pain can shoot through us so sharply—because, on a neurological level, it's experienced much like physical pain.

The attachment doesn't just stay limited to feelings of affection or companionship either. It influences how we view ourselves and our value in the world. An emotional attachment often shapes our identity, especially in long-term relationships. When that attachment breaks, it's like losing a part of your own story. You suddenly find yourself wrestling with questions: Who am I without this person? Am I still worthy of love? Such existential doubts can spiral, adding layers to the emotional weight.

Understanding these dynamics brings clarity to what can feel overwhelmingly chaotic. It's not about weakness or failure; it's about how deeply we're built to bond. These attachments grow whenever partners share vulnerability, dreams, or face life's challenges together. It's this interdependence that makes detaching so difficult. You aren't just grieving a person, but the web of emotions built around them—trust, hope, intimacy, and the feeling of being truly known.

One key aspect of emotional attachment is the interplay between reliance and autonomy. Healthy attachments allow both partners to feel secure enough to be independent yet connected. After a breakup, the balance is dramatically disrupted. The safe space where vulnerability was welcomed might now feel like a void echoing with loneliness. The withdrawal symptoms of this lost connection can mimic addiction, which explains why thoughts of an ex can invade your mind so persistently. Your brain craves the neurochemical rewards—the dopamine rush linked to love and closeness—that it received during the relationship.

It's entirely natural to want to fill that emptiness quickly, sometimes by clinging to hope for reconciliation or by trying to maintain a connection through digital channels. However, this clinging often prolongs distress. Emotional attachments are complicated by the fact that they're not purely rational; they bypass the logical parts of the brain and take residence in the emotional centers. That's why telling yourself to "just move on" rarely works—it requires more than willpower. True healing means acknowledging these attachments and gently loosening their grip without force.

The attachment framework explains why ambivalence after a breakup is common. You might find yourself vacillating between wanting to hold on and recognizing that it's time to let go. This hesitation is part of the brain's effort to recalibrate—to find new sources of emotional nourishment and security. It's a gradual, often bumpy process, where feelings of pain coexist with small moments of relief and empowerment.

It's important to remember that emotional attachments vary in intensity and form. Not all bonds are secure; some dwell in anxiety or avoidance, which complicates breakup recovery further. For example, if your attachment style leans toward anxious, you might experience greater fear of abandonment, leading to more intense heartbreak. Recognizing your attachment style doesn't excuse painful reactions but helps you understand why they surface so strongly and teaches you how to foster healthier connections moving forward.

The more we understand emotional attachments, the more equipped we become to treat ourselves kindly during this vulnerable time. Instead of blaming your emotions or judging yourself for the pain, you can hold those feelings with compassion. Emotional attachments aren't mistakes or flaws—they're reflective of our human need to connect deeply. You're simply experiencing the natural fallout of that bond breaking.

Breaking free from emotional attachments often requires creating new experiences that renew your sense of identity and security outside the relationship. This might mean nurturing friendships, rediscovering passions, or even simply learning to sit with your feelings without distraction. Every small step toward self-reliance chips away at the old attachment, gradually reshaping your internal landscape.

In recognizing how emotional attachments shape the ache of loss, you gain a powerful vantage point. It allows you to shift from being a passive victim of heartbreak to an active participant in your healing. You start to understand that the intensity of your pain is a testament to the depth of your connection, not a sign that you're weak or broken. This perspective fosters resilience, making it easier to hold on to hope for new beginnings.

Emotional attachments also emphasize the need for boundaries during recovery. To untangle yourself cleanly means sometimes stepping away completely, so new neural pathways and routines can establish themselves without constant reminders of the past. This is why practices like no-contact are recommended—they give your brain the space it needs to reset, disengage the emotional triggers, and start the healing process.

Moreover, understanding emotional attachments helps you realize that healing isn't about erasing memories or feelings; it's about integrating them into your story without letting them define your present or future. It teaches patience as your emotional landscape evolves and helps you accept the flux of feelings as part of growth. You learn that you don't have to rush the process, nor fight it. Instead, you can move forward gently, armed with knowledge about why it hurts so much and what you need to do to heal.

Finally, this understanding opens the door to healthier future relationships. By unpacking how your emotional attachments formed and functioned, you can identify patterns that no longer serve you and begin to build bonds founded on mutual respect, secure attachment, and emotional honesty. The pain of losing one love can become the soil from which a stronger, more authentic love eventually grows.

Don't Text Them—What to Do Instead

When a relationship ends, the urge to reach out through texts can feel overwhelming, but resisting that impulse is one of the most compassionate acts you can offer yourself. Instead of opening a channel that often prolongs confusion and pain, focus on redirecting your energy toward grounding practices that nurture your well-being. This might mean stepping into moments of silence to listen to your feelings without distraction or engaging in activities that remind you of your own worth and identity outside the relationship. It's not about avoiding closure—it's about creating a space where healing can truly begin, free from the back-and-forth that usually thwarts progress. By choosing not to text, you reclaim control over your emotions and begin crafting a future untethered from past attachments, setting the stage for genuine growth and clarity.

Setting Boundaries After The Breakup is a crucial step that often gets overlooked in the whirlwind of emotions that follow the end of a relationship. When you're freshly navigating the aftermath, it might feel natural to reach out—text, call, or check in—hoping to find some sense of familiarity or comfort. But setting firm boundaries after the breakup is exactly what empowers you to reclaim your space, sanity, and emotional well-being. This isn't about punishment or bitterness; it's about creating the conditions you need to heal and grow.

35

One of the first, and probably hardest, boundaries to establish is communication—or rather, the lack of it. After a breakup, it's common to crave contact, to want to say one more thing or clarify what went wrong. But restraint here isn't just a matter of self-control; it's a foundational act of self-respect. You allow yourself the crucial time away from the emotional rollercoaster your ex's messages might trigger. Boundaries around no texting, no calls, and definitely no spontaneous visits help keep turmoil at bay.

Setting boundaries means being honest about what you need—and then sticking to it. That might mean telling your ex directly, "I need space to process this, so I won't be responding for a while." Sometimes, a simple declaration sets the tone for mutual respect. Other times, it won't be acknowledged or respected. In those cases, reinforcing your limits isn't just advisable; it's non-negotiable. This may sound harsh, especially if you still care deeply, but without these clear boundaries, you risk slipping back into old patterns that prevent both healing and closure.

It's important to remember that boundaries after a breakup are fluid. What you start with today might shift over time as your emotional needs evolve. Initially, a blackout period with zero contact might be necessary. Weeks or months later, you might feel comfortable easing back into some form of communication—if that's what you want. The key is that these changes happen on your terms, not because you feel pressured or led by another's expectations.

Physical space plays a critical role too. This can mean separate living arrangements but also extends to social situations and online presence. If you keep seeing your ex at mutual hangouts without a plan to emotionally guard yourself, setting boundaries might involve politely excusing yourself or limiting attendance at certain events. Taking control of your environment helps lower unexpected emotional triggers and supports steady healing. Social media, in particular, is a minefield. Unfollowing, muting, or even blocking temporarily isn't cruel—it's self-care. It stops you from reopening wounds again and again.

Another big part of setting boundaries is managing shared connections. Mutual friends can unintentionally become messengers, or you might get caught in the middle of gossip or emotional updates. It's okay, even wise, to ask friends to hold off on sharing details about your ex or the breakup. Protecting your peace means you're not relying on secondhand information that might unsettle you. Surround yourself with people who respect your healing journey rather than fueling conflict or confusion.

For some, boundaries also involve renegotiating commitments like finances, shared property, or co-parenting responsibilities. These practical matters can become emotional battlegrounds if not handled with clear, calm agreements. Firm boundaries here breed security. Setting expectations for communication methods, timelines, and responsibilities creates a framework where both parties know what to expect. This structure reduces anxiety and the temptation to reach out impulsively for updates or reassurance.

Now, why is all of this boundary setting tied so closely to "Don't Text Them—What to Do Instead"? Because breaking the habit of using texting or calls as emotional lifelines is transformational. This shift forces you to find healthier outlets. Instead of reaching for your phone to seek answers or comfort, you can channel your energy into self-reflection, creative expression, or leaning on a support network that lifts you up.

Boundaries also redefine your relationship with yourself. When you say no to that impulsive text or deleted number, you're actually saying yes to self-prioritization. This boundary creates room for clarity, for feeling your feelings without distraction or interference. It also gives your brain the chance to unfog itself—allowing rational thought to catch up to the emotional flood. That clarity is essential before you can make any meaningful decisions about your future.

There might be moments when you question your boundaries, wondering if you're being too rigid or if you're missing out on "closure" by not having that last conversation. Closure, however, isn't really found through dialogue with the other person—it's something you craft within yourself. Firm boundaries keep you from revisiting the past unnecessarily and instead help you nurture the emotional distance needed to actually achieve peace of mind.

In many ways, boundary-setting is an act of courage. It asks you to face discomfort head-on—to feel the loneliness and uncertainty without immediately trying to patch it with contact or familiarity. That's why applying boundaries successfully often requires support from trusted friends, therapists, or even journaling as a tool for working through those raw feelings. It's okay to ask for help—it's a sign of strength, not weakness.

Remember, boundaries aren't about controlling the other person; they're about controlling your own environment and emotional input. This distinction is vital. You can't dictate how an ex behaves, but you can decide how much of their presence you allow into your world. This reclaiming of autonomy is itself deeply healing and empowering.

Many people find that after setting clear boundaries, they experience a shift in their overall energy and mindset. The relentless obsession ebbs, the emotional whiplash steadies, and a newfound sense of possibility takes root. Boundaries create safe zones where you can rediscover who you are outside the relationship. They clear space for growth, joy, and new love—when the time is right.

In practice, setting boundaries might mean deleting old messages, blocking numbers, or telling yourself "I will not respond if they reach out." It can also involve physical gestures like changing your routine so you don't accidentally run into your ex or asking friends not to share details about their life. Each boundary, though small it may seem, is a brick in the foundation of your healing.

The benefits extend far beyond the immediate relief from emotional pain. By defining and enforcing your limits after a breakup, you set a precedent for all future relationships. You learn to respect your own needs first and establish what healthy interaction looks like, even post-relationship. These lessons are invaluable lifelong skills that keep you centered and emotionally literate.

Setting boundaries isn't about closure alone; it's about transformation. It's about learning to sit with discomfort without running for the phone, forging a path back to yourself, and ultimately, choosing peace over chaos. This part of the breakup recovery journey is perhaps the most empowering phase. It's when you start to sense your own strength, realize you can say no and mean it, and feel the profound freedom that comes with honoring your heart's true needs.

In summary, setting boundaries after the breakup is not just a suggestion; it's a necessary act of self-preservation and self-love. It's the cornerstone that supports everything else in the healing process—from gaining clarity to rebuilding your identity. So when you feel the urge to reach out, pause and ask yourself what you're really seeking. Often, the better answer lies in honoring your boundaries and redirecting that energy inward.

Through this, you gradually rebuild a life that is yours again—not defined by anyone else's expectations or actions. And that's where real healing begins.

No Contact: The Power Move for Peace stands as an essential pillar in the landscape of healing after a breakup, especially when tangled emotions tempt you to reach out or seek answers through texting. It's probably the most effective boundary you can set—not just for the sake of moving on but to regain your sense of peace and clarity. No contact might sound simple at first, but it's a radical act of self-care that demands courage, discipline, and a deep trust in your own healing process.

After a breakup, it's natural to want to clarify things, apologize, or even just say 'hi' to see if there's any chance left. But each message you send, or read, pulls you back into a cycle of emotional turmoil, second-guessing, and lingering hope that blocks real closure. No contact cuts through all that noise by creating a boundary that protects your heart and mind. It's like hitting the reset button on your emotional state, allowing the rawness of loss to gradually soften and your thoughts to become less clouded by the other person's presence.

Choosing no contact can feel like a power move, but it's not about control or punishment directed at your ex. Rather, it's about reclaiming your own power and focusing solely on yourself. When you halt communication, you stop investing emotional energy into someone who might not be meeting your needs, or worse, someone who's keeping you stuck in a painful loop. This break from interaction is a conscious declaration that your well-being, your healing, and your future happiness come first.

You might ask, how long does no contact need to last to be effective? The answer varies per person and situation, but experts often suggest a minimum of 30 days without any form of contact—this includes texts, calls, social media messages, and even stalking their profiles online. Think of this period as a detox for your heart and mind, where you intentionally step away not just physically, but mentally too. That break will help reduce your emotional dependence and give you room to rediscover who you are without your ex's influence.

One of the hardest parts of no contact is resisting the urge to check on what your ex is doing. The temptation to scroll through their photos or see if they've moved on can feel like quick relief from pain, but it's usually a trap that drags you deeper into emotional chaos. Be gentle with yourself if you slip up, but also try to recognize those moments as signs you still need this boundary in place. Protecting your emotional well-being involves more than just silence—it requires vigilance over how you engage with memories and reminders.

It's worth noting that no contact isn't a blanket solution for every breakup scenario. In some cases, especially where children, shared living spaces, or unavoidable responsibilities are involved, complete no contact isn't possible. But even then, establishing strict and clear boundaries within whatever communication is necessary can mimic the benefits of no contact. Limiting conversation to specific topics, setting times when communication happens, or using third-party mediators can all serve to preserve your emotional space while managing practical realities.

During the no-contact phase, your focus should turn inward. This is the time to listen closely to your own needs, moods, and desires. Instead of spending energy on texting or wondering what could've been, channel that curiosity and emotional bandwidth into activities that rebuild and strengthen you. Write in a journal, pick up new hobbies you put aside, or simply rest. Each small action that nurtures your well-being helps stitch the wounds left by the breakup.

This period also shines a light on patterns and habits worth reevaluating. Why did you keep texting or reaching out before? Was it fear of loneliness, a hope for reconciliation, or perhaps the need for validation? Facing those underlying feelings head-on allows you to grow stronger, making it less likely that you'll fall back into old cycles the next time something painful happens. No contact isn't merely a pause. It's a chance to press 'play' on a healthier, wiser way of relating to love and loss.

It's important to remember that no contact is not about erasing the past or pretending the relationship never existed. It's a pause that lets you honor what was— what you loved, what you learned, and what you're ready to leave behind. Once the emotional dust settles, you can revisit memories with a clearer heart and a sense of gratitude rather than pain. That's a powerful transition, and no contact helps you get there.

The emotional benefits of no contact extend beyond just minimizing hurt feelings. With distance, your brain begins to rewire emotional connections. The intense attachment hormones and stress your body cranked out start to subside. As those cycles calm, you regain the cognitive space for perspective and wisdom. Suddenly, breakup pain isn't as overwhelming, and hope for future happiness becomes more realistic instead of desperate.

Some might worry that no contact comes off as cold or distant to their ex. That's understandable because breaking habits of closeness feels unnatural, but it's crucial to realize that your emotional health matters more than someone else's expectations. You get to set the tone for your healing journey. Besides, in many cases, this space prompts healthier dynamics later on—whether that means genuine closure or even friendship down the road, but only on your terms.

If you find yourself struggling to commit to no contact, try to remember what you're really aiming for: peace. That elusive, quiet feeling where your heart no longer races at the thought of 'what if.' No contact is the clean slate that makes peace possible. It's a bold, boundary-filled way to say: I'm choosing myself, I'm choosing healing, and I'm ready to move forward without being pulled backward by old narratives.

By embracing no contact, you also honor the truth that healing isn't linear or instantaneous. Some days you'll feel stronger; others, more vulnerable. The point is that stepping away from the temptation to communicate helps you maintain a compass focused on self-respect and growth rather than regret or resentment. Over time, this builds resilience, confidence, and a renewed capacity for love that's healthier and more fulfilling.

To sum it up, no contact is a strategic loving act toward yourself. It might be uncomfortable and counterintuitive at first, especially when you're aching for connection. But the peace you create in that space becomes the foundation for the next chapter of your life—a chapter where you're empowered, clear, and ready to embrace the possibilities ahead.

- Set a clear no-contact period (start with 30 days) and communicate it if needed for mutual respect.

- Remove triggers: unfollow or mute your ex on social media to reduce temptation.
- Focus on self-care and activities that rebuild your identity, outside the shadow of the relationship.
- Recognize emotional triggers and replace the urge to text with journaling or talking to trusted friends.
- Be patient with yourself; healing through no contact is a journey, not a quick fix.

This power move—choosing no contact—is one of the truest ways to reclaim your story and make peace with your past. It opens the doorway to rediscover your worth unburdened by the relationship's end. That's real strength. That's real freedom.

CHAPTER 2

THE HEALING PROCESS

Healing after a breakup isn't about rushing through the pain or pretending it doesn't exist—it's about leaning into those raw feelings so you can come out clearer and stronger on the other side. It means creating safe spaces where you can truly grieve without judgment, whether that's through quiet reflection, journaling, or honest conversations with trusted friends. Letting go is a delicate balancing act; you hold on to the parts of yourself that make you whole while gently releasing what no longer serves you, including forgiveness that frees your heart without opening old wounds. This phase also calls for detoxing your mind and your digital world—sorting through memories, setting boundaries with social media, and reclaiming your mental clarity so your thoughts aren't clouded by constant reminders. Healing is not linear, but each small step you take toward feeling, letting go, and clearing your space builds a foundation for growth you can trust, paving the way for renewed strength and grace in your next chapter.

Feeling It to Heal It

Grieving the end of a relationship means allowing yourself to truly feel the full spectrum of emotions that come with loss—pain, anger, confusion, and even relief—without rushing to push them aside or numb the experience. This isn't about wallowing endlessly, but about embracing the discomfort as a necessary step toward genuine healing. When you lean into these feelings instead of avoiding them, you start to untangle the complex emotions that tie you to what was, giving you permission to process and release them. It's in this raw and honest encounter with your emotions that real recovery begins, because healing doesn't come from forgetting or suppressing your pain but from fully acknowledging it and letting it move through you. This intentional feeling-to-healing cycle creates the foundation to rebuild your life with clarity, strength, and an empowered sense of closure.

Safe Spaces to Grieve Effectively Creating a safe space to truly feel your emotions after a breakup isn't just helpful—it's essential. When a relationship ends, the flood of feelings can be overwhelming. You might feel lost, angry, numb, or a confusing mix of everything at once. But without a sanctuary where these emotions can flow freely without judgment, healing becomes harder. Safe spaces provide the permission to feel deeply, surrender vulnerability, and begin the process of emotional repair.

What exactly makes a space "safe" for grieving? It's not just about the physical environment, though that matters. A safe space is a container where your heart and mind can rest without criticism, self-blame, or pressure to "move on" before you're ready. This can be a cozy corner in your home, a favorite quiet park bench, or even a place within your own mind cultivated through meditation or mindfulness. The key is trust—trust that here, your feelings will be honored rather than dismissed.

Remember, grieving a breakup isn't a linear journey or a neat set of tasks to check off—it's messy, unpredictable, and intensely personal. Having a place (internal or external) where you feel secure enough to experience that messiness is one of the most radical acts of self-care you can practice. When you allow yourself a safe space, you're telling your mind and body that it's okay to be exactly where you are emotionally, without shame or urgency.

Sometimes, the safe spaces you create aren't just physical. They can be found in the company of compassionate friends, family members, or support groups that honor your experience without trying to fix it. Being able to speak your truth—or simply sit in silence with others who understand—can reinforce that your pain is real and valid. This shared vulnerability reassures

49

your heart that you're not alone, even in what may feel like the loneliest moments.

But safe spaces can also be incredibly solitary. Everyone's emotional needs are different. Some find peace in journaling in a quiet room, pouring raw feelings onto the page without restraint. Others find relief in creative outlets—painting, music, or movement—that open channels for expression words can't touch. These solitary practices become your personal refuge, a way to release heaviness while keeping yourself grounded. In these moments, your safe space is your emotional sanctuary, crafted by your own hands and heart.

Think about your daily life. Where do you naturally feel most at ease? Is there a spot that puts you at peace just by sitting there, maybe with a cup of tea or your favorite book? These locations can transform into intentional sites of healing when you dedicate time to simply "be" in your grief. No pushing, no distractions, no expectations— just presence. The freedom to express sadness, anger, relief, or confusion in these spaces is transformative. It legitimizes your emotions instead of burying them.

Creating this kind of environment might take conscious effort at first. You may need to communicate boundaries with those around you, letting them know when you need space or when you might need someone to listen without advice. This clarity helps reduce external pressure to "get over it" and carves out a respectful atmosphere where your healing unfolds at your rhythm. You deserve to feel safe not only physically but emotionally and mentally.

It's also important to recognize when your current environment doesn't serve your healing. Sometimes, a breakup will leave your home or regular hangouts loaded with reminders that hurt too much. In these cases, changing your surroundings temporarily can create the breathing room necessary to grieve without constant triggers. This might mean visiting a friend's place, spending more time outside, or even booking a short retreat where you can connect with your feelings without interruption.

Technology brings both challenges and blessings for creating safe spaces. On one hand, it connects you to supportive communities, counselors, or resources that can guide you through grief. On the other, scrolling social media or revisiting old messages can reopen wounds repeatedly. Managing digital exposure carefully— perhaps by muting certain accounts or setting specific times to check your phone—can protect your emotional space. Consider this part of your healing sanctuary: a digital detox zone that shelters your fragile heart.

Within your safe space, give yourself permission to experience every emotion in its fullest. Crying, screaming, laughing, or sitting in silence—all of these reactions are valid and necessary. The safety you've cultivated becomes the secure ground underneath challenging feelings. Instead of pushing pain underground, where it festers, your grief can flow through you and eventually begin to ease.

What's often forgotten is that effective grieving isn't just about releasing pain—it's about making room for new hope. Safe spaces offer that dual purpose. They become places where you can gently transition from heartbreak to healing, from loss to rediscovery. In time, these environments nurture resilience, self-compassion, and clarity. They remind you that your story hasn't ended with the breakup; it's simply the beginning of a new chapter.

A safe space also invites patience. Healing isn't a linear path nor a race to an endpoint. The safe spaces you build slow down the process to something much more human. They hold the tension between honoring your pain and trusting that you will one day rebuild stronger than before. Resting here allows you to rebuild the foundation of your emotional life carefully, rather than rushing toward a superficial "closure" that never really sticks.

Finally, remember that you alone define what safety looks like for you. Your safe space might change over time, evolving as your feelings shift and your needs grow. The power lies in your ability to recognize and nurture these spaces repeatedly. The more you protect and prioritize these environments, the easier it becomes to feel your feelings honestly—and that honest feeling is the heart of healing.

Grieving effectively demands not only feeling but also trusting the conditions that allow feeling without harm. Creating and guarding your safe spaces gives you just that: a compassionate home for your heartbreak. It's within these spaces that you begin to shed what no longer serves you and open up to the possibility of love—whether for yourself or others—once again.

Journaling Prompts for Emotional Release
After a breakup, feeling the swirl of emotions can feel overwhelming. That's where journaling steps in—as a quiet, patient companion willing to meet you wherever you are. It's one of the most effective ways to give voice to feelings you may otherwise try to suppress or ignore. Writing not only helps untangle the messy knots inside but also allows a safe release for hurt, anger, confusion, and even moments of unexpected clarity. The act of putting pen to paper creates a container for emotions, especially in the pivotal "Feeling It to Heal It" phase.

To begin, you don't have to write beautifully or in full sentences. The goal isn't perfection—it's expression. If your hands tremble or your words feel stuck, that's okay. Journaling provides a pressure-free zone to let your heart speak without judgment. When you engage with yourself honestly on the page, you create space to process your pain instead of running from it. Below are thoughtfully crafted journal prompts designed specifically to ease your path through emotional release after a breakup, helping you connect with your truest feelings and eventually find clearer ground.

Start with something simple to check in with where you are right now. For example, "What emotion is the loudest in me today?" or "What sensation in my body is telling me how I'm feeling?" Holding curiosity for whatever surfaces—even if it's just numbness—allows your internal landscape to unfold. When you acknowledge your emotions without pushing them away, you honor your experience instead of silencing it.

Moving deeper, try prompts that explore the stories you tell yourself about the breakup. Ask, "What story have I been telling myself about why this relationship ended? What parts might not be entirely true?" This helps separate emotional reactions from the narratives you may have unconsciously created to explain your pain. When you hold those stories with a questioning mindset, they lose some of their power to trap you in hurt and open space for honest reflection.

Another useful prompt encourages expressing anger or hurt directly. Write out, "If I could say everything to my ex without stopping, what would I say?" or "What resentments am I holding on to, and how do they affect me?" Pouring these feelings onto the page can be incredibly cathartic, especially when you find it hard to voice them aloud. It's a way of owning your anger while gently controlling it rather than letting it control you.

Grief often hides underneath other emotions like frustration or sadness. Use journaling to sit with grief by exploring prompts such as, "What parts of this relationship do I mourn the most?" or "What am I losing that feels precious to me?" Naming specific losses can bring a sigh of relief because grief becomes less nebulous and more tangible. This is a critical step in "Feeling It to Heal It" because acknowledging your grief is what makes healing possible.

Sometimes your mind is a storm of "what ifs" and regrets. When you find yourself caught in that cycle, journaling can help realign your focus. Try prompts like, "What lessons did this relationship teach me about myself?" or "How have I grown even in the midst of pain?" These questions shine light on your resilience and growth, recognizing that healing involves both feeling deeply and learning from what happened.

Self-compassion is often a missing piece in breakup recovery. Many of us become our own harshest critics when heartache hits. Journaling prompts such as, "What would I say to a friend going through this same pain?" or "How can I be kinder to myself today?" encourage a tender inner voice. Writing this way softens self-judgment and invites patience, acceptance, and love—qualities essential to rebuilding after loss.

Here's an invitation to explore your future through your journal: "What kind of life do I want to create now that I'm free from this relationship?" or "What boundaries do

55

I want to set moving forward to protect my well-being?" These prompts shift your perspective away from what's been lost toward what you're gaining—your autonomy and the chance to redefine yourself on your own terms.

It's natural to feel stuck or resistant to journaling, especially when emotions feel volatile. One approach is to give yourself permission to write messily or even to scribble words and doodles without structure. The important part is showing up—even in small ways—and letting the process unfold organically. Sometimes just sitting with a simple prompt like, "Today, I feel..." can become a breakthrough.

Journaling can also be combined with other forms of emotional release. After writing, you might choose to read aloud what you've written or tear up pages as a symbolic gesture of releasing pain. These physical acts reinforce the emotional work, helping you feel heard both within yourself and in your body. In the same way, you may find writing letters to your ex—without the intention to send—offers liberation and closure you might not have accessed through conversation.

Remember, journaling isn't about rushing to "fix" your feelings or to produce neat insights quickly. It's a container for your truth in all its rawness. Over time, you may notice your journal entries shift from confusion and pain toward acceptance and clarity. The transformation isn't always linear, and that's normal. Some days the words flow effortlessly; on others, the page seems stubbornly blank. Both are part of the healing journey.

Engaging consistently with these journaling prompts nurtures a deeper self-awareness and emotional fluency. As your relationship with your own feelings matures, you'll find it easier to embrace vulnerability and let go of what no longer serves you. In turn, this clarity becomes the foundation for the freedom and resilience that this chapter promises.

Lastly, consider revisiting past journal entries after some time has passed. Re-reading your reflections can show you how far you've come, reveal patterns you didn't realize, and reinforce the work you've done. It's also a reminder that even in heartbreak, there is growth, wisdom, and the quiet promise of healing. Each word you write is a step toward reclaiming your story with power, grace, and hope.

Letting Go, Not Losing Yourself

Letting go after a breakup doesn't mean erasing who you are or becoming unrecognizable to yourself— it's about reclaiming your sense of self beyond the relationship's story. This process invites you to untangle the parts of your identity that got wrapped up in someone else, to find the core of who you truly are independent of the shared past. It's natural to feel lost or unsure at first, but by embracing this space, you create room for growth rather than emptiness. The challenge lies in releasing attachment without sacrificing your worth or values, learning that goodbye can be a step toward rediscovering what makes you whole. Holding onto your authentic self is not just a balm for pain—it's the foundation for rebuilding stronger, clearer, and ready to move forward with confidence.

Separating Identity From The Relationship is one of the most delicate yet crucial steps when you're navigating the aftermath of a breakup. It might sound simple on the surface—just move on, right? But the truth is, your identity often becomes so intertwined with your partner and the relationship dynamic that untangling yourself feels like trying to pull apart two pieces of chewed gum. When a relationship ends, it can feel like not only has your world shifted, but a part of who you believed yourself to be has fractured, too. In this sub-section, we'll explore how to gently reclaim your sense of self without losing the love and lessons the relationship gave you.

When we're in relationships, our identities don't exist in a vacuum. They get woven into shared experiences, routines, and even the way we view ourselves. Maybe you were "the couple who always did weekend hikes," or the person whose favorite hobby was tied to what you and your partner enjoyed together. Over time, these shared identities can become so familiar that when the relationship ends, it feels like losing a layer of yourself. The challenge is learning how to recognize where your core identity ends and where the relationship's influence begins—because only then can you begin to rebuild who you are on your own terms.

This process isn't about denying the meaningful parts of your past relationship or pretending it never shaped you—it absolutely did, and it should. But it's about understanding that your value and your sense of who you are doesn't solely depend on who you were with in that relationship. That separating line can be blurry, and it takes patience and compassion to find it. You'll want to look honestly at what parts of your life and self were nurtured or changed because of the relationship, versus what parts were intrinsically yours from the start.

One way to approach this is to start noticing the small things you do and enjoy independently. What activities make you feel alive when you're alone? What beliefs and values have stayed steady through the ups and downs of that partnership? Often, it helps to make lists or journal your feelings. Write about your hopes, interests, and dreams that existed before the relationship or even things you feel emerging anew now. These can act as a map, guiding you back toward a centered and authentic you.

It's also important to dismantle the idea that your identity is somehow "locked" in your role within the relationship. You might have been a partner, a co-parent, a teammate—but those roles, while significant, don't fully define you. The loss of these roles can feel jarring because they come packed with purpose and connection. Yet, they're roles that can be redefined and expanded upon, not erased. How do you reclaim your life beyond those relationship labels? It starts with asking yourself who you want to be, separate from any external attachment or expectation.

Embracing this separate self can feel uncomfortable, especially at first. There's often fear: fear of loneliness, fear of being incomplete, or fear of making choices without the relationship's influence. But these fears are part of the healing journey—they signal that you're stepping outside your comfort zone and forging a new path. Lean into this discomfort rather than shying away from it. In doing so, you'll find a growing well of inner strength and clarity that becomes the foundation of your post-breakup life.

Another vital piece of this process involves setting boundaries with your former partner, your shared environment, and even your own mind. For example, limiting contact or redefining your relationship's place in your social circles and daily habits can give you the mental and emotional space to reshape your identity. When you continue interacting in the same patterns that blurred your individuality, you risk stalling your growth. Physical, emotional, and digital boundaries help you reclaim the space you need to rediscover who you are and who you want to become.

Sometimes, identity entanglement shows up as a constant "blur" of past and present, where you catch yourself repeating phrases like "we used to..." or "when we did this..." This ongoing mental looping can keep you stuck as if living in the shadows of your previous relationship. To break free, mindfulness and self-compassion are your allies. When these thoughts arise, gently acknowledge them without judgment, and then bring your focus back to your current life, your current self. Over time, this repeated practice quiets the noise of your intertwined identity and strengthens the boundaries that separate past from now.

It's also normal to question your self-worth or feel like a part of you is "broken" after a breakup. Separating your identity from the relationship doesn't mean perfect confidence will instantly blossom—or even that you'll always feel whole right away. Healing is more about learning to accept your vulnerabilities and seeing your worth independent of your relationship status. Your value as a person isn't a reflection of the partnership's success or failure; it's rooted deeply in who you are beyond anyone else. This mindset shift requires time and gentle reaffirmation.

Building rituals that celebrate your individuality can be transformative in solidifying your separate identity. Maybe it's starting a new hobby, re-immersing yourself in old passions, or setting aside quiet moments for self-reflection each day. These rituals act as tangible reminders that your life is yours to curate and cherish. They also serve as stepping stones toward emotional independence—the ability to feel complete on your own, not waiting for someone else to "complete" you.

In the process of separation, it's essential not to rush or force yourself into a completely new identity overnight. Allow yourself to oscillate between moments of sorrow, nostalgia, hope, and excitement. These emotions are part and parcel of detangling who you were tied to and who you're becoming. What matters most is that the arc of your journey bends towards reclamation and empowerment, even if it's a winding path with detours along the way.

Remember, separating your identity from the relationship isn't an act of erasing your shared story but rather honoring your individual chapters yet to be written. The healing process here is one of rediscovery and rebirth. As you gently rebuild your sense of self, you'll find that you're not losing the past—you're integrating it into a stronger, more resilient you. This reclaimed identity becomes the solid ground for future love, deeper self-trust, and an unshakable inner peace that no relationship alone can define.

Forgiveness Without Reconnection is one of the most challenging—and yet profoundly liberating—steps you'll encounter on your healing journey. It's about learning to release the heavy burden of resentment, anger, or pain toward someone without feeling the need to reopen lines of communication or re-establish a bond. This kind of forgiveness isn't about condoning what happened or pretending the wounds don't exist. Instead, it's about choosing peace for yourself, setting down the emotional baggage, and reclaiming your power without inviting someone back into your life who no longer fits your growth.

When a relationship ends, especially a romantic one, it's natural to want answers, closure, or maybe even a fresh start. But messy, complicated emotions often muddy the waters. You might think that forgiving someone means reconnecting, talking through every issue, or even becoming friends. The truth is, forgiveness is inward—it's your gift to yourself, independent of what the other person does or doesn't do. It frees you from being tethered to the pain their actions caused. If you hang on to the bitterness or keep revisiting old wounds, it's like dragging around an anchor that sinks you deeper into sorrow and stagnation.

Forgiveness without reconnection respects your boundaries and your right to heal fully on your terms. Not every love story deserves a sequel. Holding on to hope for a second chance can trap you in emotional limbo, causing continued confusion and preventing wholehearted healing. Sometimes, the healthiest and bravest choice is to forgive from a distance—and that distance might have to be absolute. You might not be ready for this at first, and that's okay. True forgiveness is never rushed. It unfolds gently as your heart mends and you begin to see yourself clearly again, apart from the person who hurt you.

Imagine forgiveness as a form of emotional decluttering. You're sorting through your feelings, acknowledging the hurt and betrayal without letting them define you or your future. Letting go doesn't mean you're weak or forgetful. It means you're refusing to carry unnecessary weight that smothers your joy and potential for growth. It means affirming that your worth isn't tied to someone else's mistakes or decisions. And here's the most powerful part: forgiveness without reconnection allows you to reclaim your story—one where you're the author, not a reluctant reader stuck on a painful chapter.

It helps to recognize that forgiveness is a process, often nonlinear and unique to your experience. Some days you might feel ready; others, anger or sorrow might flare up fiercely. This back-and-forth is natural. What matters is your commitment to keep trying. Sometimes, writing down your feelings or talking them through with a trusted confidant or therapist can clarify your journey. When you look honestly at what you're forgiving—whether it's betrayal, neglect, or something else—you begin to dismantle the power those wounds held over you.

Forgiveness without reconnection also guards your emotional boundaries. By forgiving at arm's length, you protect yourself from reopening wounds or falling back into unhealthy patterns. It's about placing your well-being first. Forgiving doesn't mean you're opening your door for someone to hurt you again, nor does it mean you have to maintain any ongoing relationship, whether cordial or otherwise. You're acknowledging what happened and then deliberately choosing peace over pain, which empowers you to stay true to your needs.

For many, the hardest part is the societal or internalized pressure to reconcile—to "make peace" by reconnecting in some form. There's often a misconception that forgiveness equates to friendship or even romantic revival. But mixing forgiveness with reconnection before you're actually ready—or before it's genuinely safe—can lead to confusion and emotional setbacks. Your healing won't thrive on premature contact. Instead, it flourishes in clarity, self-respect, and the quiet strength of knowing you don't have to relive the past to move on.

Another important element is recognizing that forgiveness without reconnection isn't about denying the lessons or complexities of the relationship. It's a perspective shift. Instead of replaying the "what ifs" or falling into bitterness, you acknowledge the experience as a chapter of growth, not a measure of your value. You honor the feelings you had and allowed yourself to be vulnerable, but you leave behind the pain that no longer serves you. This mindset releases you to step into a future that's unburdened by old wounds.

Some people worry that forgiving someone—even silently—might feel like letting them "off the hook."

But forgiveness is about your emancipation, not their absolution. You don't owe someone your emotional labor or validation, especially if they caused harm. By forgiving without reconnecting, you're refusing to be defined by past hurt. You're choosing to live with a lighter heart that's free to nurture new beginnings, rather than dragging the shadows of a broken love behind you.

Consider the metaphor of a house that's been damaged by a storm. Forgiveness without reconnection is like cleaning up the debris inside, fixing the cracks, and repainting the walls—not inviting the storm back through the door. It's a way to restore your inner home to a place of safety and warmth, without inviting chaos or unpredictability back in. It's entirely possible to forgive someone and remain distance protectors of your emotional sanctuary at the same time.

There's healing in recognizing your control over the narrative—what parts you keep, what parts you let go of, and how you define your future relationships. Forgiveness without reconnection is a testament to your self-worth and resilience. It's a declaration that your healing journey need not be contingent on rekindling or re-engaging with someone who's no longer aligned with your growth. You get to set the terms.

Practicing forgiveness at a distance also fosters compassion toward yourself. Sometimes, the hardest forgiveness is the one you need to offer yourself for staying too long in people-pleasing patterns or ignoring red flags. By separating forgiveness from reconnection, you open space for gentleness and self-care. It reminds you that healing is messy and imperfect, and that's wholly human. You don't have to rush or rationalize your feelings to be worthy of peace.

Lastly, forgiveness without reconnection can illuminate the path to emotional freedom. It invites you to reclaim your life, rebuild your identity, and move forward without carrying the emotional weight of the past relationship. This kind of forgiveness allows love to return—not necessarily to the person who caused pain, but to yourself. It's the foundation on which you'll rebuild your trust in others, and most importantly, your trust in your own heart.

Detoxing Your Mind and Digital Life

After a breakup, your mind can feel cluttered with memories and emotions, while your digital world often keeps reminders alive in ways that make moving on harder. Clearing this space isn't about erasing your past but about creating room to breathe and heal. That might mean muting or unfollowing to protect your peace, setting limits on scrolling through old photos, or simply taking breaks from social media to avoid constant triggers. Detoxing your mind and digital life helps reclaim clarity, giving you the mental headspace needed to process your feelings fully and refocus on your healing journey. It's a compassionate act of self-care—one that empowers you to regain control over what occupies your attention and nurtures the fresh start you deserve.

Managing Social Media and Memories is a crucial part of detoxing your mind and digital life after a breakup. In today's hyper-connected world, social media often becomes an unavoidable reminder of what was lost—a constant stream of images, posts, and memories that can keep you stuck in the past. Navigating this digital landscape with intention isn't just about avoiding pain; it's about reclaiming your emotional space and setting the groundwork for genuine healing. When a relationship ends, the old photos, shared posts, and mutual friends online can feel like digital echoes of a story you're trying to close. Managing these elements thoughtfully helps you regain control over your story and experience the healing process fully.

The first step in managing social media after a breakup often involves creating boundaries that protect your emotional well-being. It's tempting to stay glued to your ex's profiles, checking for updates or scrolling through old photos. But this behavior frequently prolongs the pain and makes moving forward harder. Instead, consider what kind of interaction, if any, is healthy for you right now. For many, this means unfollowing or muting your ex on platforms like Instagram, Facebook, or Twitter without necessarily blocking them immediately. This simple act creates distance without the added drama of confrontation. It's an act of self-care that lets you start seeing your world beyond the remnants of the past relationship.

Sometimes, you might choose to take even more protective measures, such as unfriending or blocking your ex if exposure to their updates keeps reopening wounds. This isn't about running away or punishing anyone; it's about prioritizing your mental health. Remember, your digital environment significantly affects your emotional state. The constant presence of your ex online can trigger feelings ranging from sadness and jealousy to anger and regret. It's okay to curate your social media in a way that fosters healing, even if that means a temporary or permanent break from some connections.

Beyond just curating your ex's presence on your feed, managing shared memories is an essential part of this detox. Pictures, videos, messages—they're all digital souvenirs that hold emotional weight. You don't have to erase the past completely to heal, but it's important to manage how much you immerse yourself in it. Consider creating a "memory box" offline, whether physical or encrypted digital storage, where you can keep meaningful mementos safely tucked away. You might also make a private folder on your phone or computer where photos and messages from the relationship are stored but not displayed daily. This approach respects your feelings and the significance of the memories while keeping them from dominating your everyday consciousness.

It's also important to acknowledge that deleting or archiving your memories is a gradual process. The impulse to "just get rid of everything" after a breakup is strong but often impulsive. Some keepsakes may bring comfort after the initial chaos settles, so avoid making decisions driven purely by pain or anger. Healing is nonlinear, and there might be moments when revisiting some memories feels helpful rather than harmful. The goal is to have these memories on your own terms, not in a way that drags you down unexpectedly. Setting boundaries around when and how you engage with these memories empowers you to process your feelings with intention rather than becoming overwhelmed by them.

Social media doesn't just amplify memories; it often invites well-meaning—but sometimes unhelpful—input from friends and acquaintances. Comments, likes, and unsolicited advice can complicate your emotional landscape. You might find yourself defensive or caught off guard by what others say or don't say, especially soon after a breakup. Remember that your healing is personal, and the digital space is rarely a neutral playground. If it becomes a source of stress, consider limiting your interactions, turning off notifications, or even temporarily deactivating accounts. These steps aren't signs of weakness but of self-respect. Creating a social media environment that respects your needs reduces emotional noise, allowing your mind the clarity it needs to heal.

Another dimension of managing social media involves how you represent yourself moving forward. After the end of a relationship, there's often a temptation to post indirect messages, photos to signal your independence, or even to discreetly project your emotional state. While these actions may feel validating momentarily, they can slow your healing or blur the closure you seek. It's more empowering to use social media as a platform to nurture your new identity as an individual, not as someone still defined by a past relationship. Sharing content that inspires your growth, reconnecting with interests you paused, or simply allowing yourself the space to be quiet online can serve your recovery better than reactive posts or emotional outbursts.

For some, social media can also be a helpful venue to seek support and rediscovery. Joining communities or groups focused on healing, self-improvement, or creative hobbies can create positive engagement and remind you that life continues beyond your past relationship. But again, moderation is key. Balance your online time carefully so it supplements your healing rather than replaces deep, in-person coping mechanisms or reflection. Rebuilding your life requires genuine connection with yourself and others, which digital life alone cannot fulfill.

It's essential to be honest with yourself about what feels right in terms of social media usage after a breakup. Everyone's threshold for digital exposure varies, so listen to your emotional cues. If scrolling through old posts triggers anxiety or sadness, that's a clear sign to step back. Conversely, if you find joy in revisiting certain memories or posting updates about your journey, honor those feelings. Healing includes both letting go and embracing new beginnings, and your digital presence can support or hinder you based on how you navigate it.

Finally, consider that managing memories and social media is a practice, not a one-time fix. As you heal, your relationship with your digital life will evolve. There'll be phases when you're ready to unblock, reconnect, or refresh your profiles with new stories and photos. Other times, you might need to tighten limits again. This flexibility with yourself nurtures resilience and self-compassion. What matters most is your commitment to creating a digital environment that preserves your mental well-being and supports your emotional growth.

In summary, managing social media and memories during a breakup is about you reclaiming control. These platforms and digital keepsakes, once shared spaces of joy and connection, may now feel like stumbling blocks. But by thoughtfully setting boundaries, curating content, and deciding what to engage with and when, you create a nurturing digital space that facilitates rather than obstructs your healing process. The goal is clear: detox your digital life in a way that truly clears space for your heart and mind to mend, so your next chapter begins with clarity and strength.

Reclaiming Mental Clarity and Headspace is one of the most pivotal parts of detoxing your mind and digital life during the healing process. After a breakup, your mind often feels like a storm-tossed sea—turbulent, chaotic, and messy. That mental clutter doesn't just make it hard to move on; it can prevent you from fully processing what happened and setting healthy intentions for your future. Reclaiming clarity means gently clearing away the emotional and digital debris that keeps pulling your attention back to the past, so you can finally breathe and think clearly again.

When a relationship ends, your mind can become a relentless loop playing reminders, regrets, and "what ifs." This constant mental noise makes emotional space thin and keeps anxiety alive. Detoxing from that noise isn't about forcefully suppressing your feelings or pretending everything is fine—it's about intentionally carving out time and space to untangle your thoughts. It's easier said than done, but making this your focus helps you regain control over your own narrative instead of being swept away by it.

The digital world often intensifies this mental clutter. Social media highlights moments that don't reflect your full reality but can torpedo your progress if revisited repeatedly. Notifications, old photos, and even silent "likes" from your ex can act as emotional triggers. It's crucial to manage these digital touchpoints because they anchor your mind to reminders you're trying to let go of. Recognizing that your online habits have an impact on your mental health is a powerful step toward reclaiming your headspace. You have the power to create digital boundaries that protect your healing journey.

Imagine your mental clarity as a garden. When weeds—worries, ruminations, unanswered messages—are left unchecked, they crowd out the flowers you want to grow: peace, self-compassion, and hope. Clearing that garden means pruning harmful digital interactions just as much as it involves quieting the voices in your head that replay old narratives. You don't have to uproot all your memories at once. Instead, start small by removing or muting digital reminders that cause unnecessary distress, then gradually introduce other practices that help settle your mind.

In practical terms, setting aside time away from screens offers one of the most immediate benefits. It might feel uncomfortable initially, as your brain has grown used to constant digital stimulation, but it's essential for peeling back layers of mental fog. Even a few hours without checking social media or refraining from scrolling through old messages allows your mind to rest and recover, creating space for clarity to emerge naturally. During this break, journaling, meditation, or simply sitting with your thoughts without judgment can deepen that clarity even more.

Detoxing your mind also means cultivating new habits that support a calmer, focused mental state.

Mindfulness techniques help anchor you in the present moment, taking your attention away from past pain. Breathing exercises, grounding practices, or mindful walks can interrupt cycles of rumination, reminding you that your mind is more than the pain it's carrying. Over time, these small shifts add up to big changes in how you manage emotional turbulence, slowly replacing chaos with calm.

It's important to remember that reclaiming mental clarity doesn't equate to forgetting or erasing your past relationship. Instead, it's about making peace with it so it no longer holds hostage your emotional well-being. That shift in perspective happens gradually. You'll notice that moments which once felt charged with pain become more neutral, and thoughts about your ex stop triggering intense emotional reactions. Mental headspace isn't an empty void; it's a fertile ground where new ideas, passions, and even love can grow.

Another practical step involves recalibrating your digital environment. This doesn't necessarily mean a total social media blackout, though for some that might be the right move temporarily. Instead, consider curating your feeds to include uplifting, supportive content that aligns with your healing goals. Unfollow or mute accounts that feed jealousy, self-doubt, or resentment. Silence group chats that pull you back into gossip or endless discussions about what went wrong. Digital detox is a form of boundary-setting—an act of self-respect that sends a clear message to yourself and others about your priorities.

Many find it helpful to create offline rituals that serve as mental anchors. These rituals remind you that your self-worth and peace don't depend on digital validation. Whether it's reading a physical book, journaling in a favorite notebook, or engaging in a creative hobby, these activities fill your mind with purpose and positive energy. They provide a reset button when the digital world feels overwhelming or invasive. Over time, these small practices chisel away at anxiety and restore a calmer, more confident inner voice.

Still, mental clarity can sometimes feel elusive, especially when memories or emotions strike unexpectedly. That's okay. Healing is not linear, and detoxing your mind will have its ups and downs too. What matters is your commitment to creating an environment— both digital and emotional—that supports your peace instead of dismantling it. It's a daily practice of choosing what deserves your attention, patience with yourself in moments of struggle, and an openness to rediscovering who you are outside the relationship.

In essence, reclaiming mental clarity and headspace is about regaining ownership of your internal world. When you carve out the mental space needed for healing, you empower yourself to move beyond heartbreak into renewal. You'll find strength not by pushing feelings away but by welcoming them compassionately, then choosing what to carry forward and what to release. That clarity becomes the foundation on which you rebuild—clear-eyed, stronger, and with a renewed sense of self that no breakup can diminish.

CHAPTER 3

REBUILDING YOU

After the chaos of heartbreak and the rawness of healing, the next step is about intentionally reconstructing who you are outside of that old love story. This is where you become your own safe place, learning to trust yourself again and nurturing a sense of worth that isn't dependent on anyone else's approval. It's about setting clear boundaries—not just to keep toxicity out but to honor what you truly deserve—and redefining the standards that guide your relationships moving forward. Rebuilding is also a chance to rediscover passions that may have been neglected, to set goals that excite you, and to embrace transformation not only on the surface but deep inside, helping you glow with confidence and clarity. It's a courageous, active process of leveling up your life with patience and kindness toward yourself, so the new chapter that unfolds is stronger, wiser, and unapologetically you.

Becoming Your Own Safe Place

When a relationship ends, the world you once knew feels shaky, but rebuilding begins with creating safety within yourself. Becoming your own safe place means learning to trust your feelings without judgment and treating yourself with the kindness you'd offer a close friend. It's about recognizing that security isn't something only others can give you—it's something you cultivate through daily habits, honest self-reflection, and setting gentle but firm boundaries around your emotional space. This foundation lets you stand steady amid uncertainty, nurturing a sense of calm and confidence that no heartbreak can shake. By turning inward for comfort and validation, you reclaim control over your healing journey and lay the groundwork for the stronger, more resilient you who's ready for whatever comes next.

Cultivating Self-Trust and Self-Worth Daily
Becoming your own safe place starts with the foundation of self-trust and self-worth. After a breakup, especially a tough one, these two elements might feel slippery or even shattered. But rebuilding them isn't about overnight magic or some sudden leap; it's a daily commitment, a practice forged through small, intentional acts. You can't rush trust—not in others, and definitely not in yourself.

Instead, it grows when you decide, again and again, to show up for yourself with honesty, kindness, and respect.

One of the first steps in cultivating self-trust is recognizing the difference between self-doubt and healthy questioning. When you're flooded with negative voices that say you'll never be enough or question your ability to be emotionally safe for yourself, that's not a reality check—it's a distortion. Self-trust means acknowledging those doubts without letting them control you. It means giving yourself permission to feel uncertain but choosing not to freeze or run from it. It's about believing that even when you don't have all the answers, your inner compass will guide you through.

Imagine every time you keep a commitment to yourself—as simple as getting out of bed on a tough morning or telling yourself the truth about your feelings— as a brick being laid in the foundation of your self-trust. Maybe yesterday you doubted your resilience, but today you followed through on a promise to yourself, no matter how small. That action tells your mind and heart: "I am reliable. I can count on myself." When this repeats daily, those bricks stack, forming a sturdy and reliable platform from which you can navigate future challenges.

Self-worth, on the other hand, thrives on the recognition of your inherent value, independent of what you achieve or who you're with. The temptation after a breakup is to tie your worth to external validation— getting texts back, seeing your ex with someone new, or trying to prove you're "over it." But your worth isn't something to be earned through outside sources. It's built from within, a quiet declaration that you deserve love, respect, and care simply because you exist.

If you find yourself constantly measuring your worth through achievements or approval, try shifting the lens gently. Start with daily affirmations rooted not in perfection but in acceptance: "I am enough as I am today," "I deserve kindness from myself," or "I am learning and growing at my own pace." These statements might feel awkward or even false at first, but repetition rewires thought patterns. Over time, your brain will start accepting these truths as the baseline rather than the exception.

Another powerful way to deepen self-worth and trust is by setting clear boundaries—not with the goal of controlling others, but protecting your emotional energy. Every time you say no to something that doesn't serve your peace or yes to something that feels right, you send yourself a strong message. Boundaries aren't walls; they're signs pointing toward self-respect. They say, "I value my feelings and my well-being enough to advocate for them." When you act according to those boundaries, your confidence in yourself grows because you're practicing radical ownership of your needs.

Daily journaling can offer a safe space to witness this internal work. Rather than just recounting events, try diving into your feelings around trust and worth.

Ask yourself questions like, "Where did I listen to my intuition today?" or "What moment made me feel proud of standing up for myself?" When you write down your answers without judgment, you're training your mind to notice progress. Over time, these reflections document your growth in soulful detail, making the intangible gains more tangible and real.

Don't underestimate the impact of small rituals designed to honor yourself. Maybe it's a morning stretch where you set an intention to be gentle with yourself. Maybe it's lighting a candle each night while repeating a phrase like, "I am safe within myself." These moments might seem insignificant in isolation, but their power comes from consistency. They reinforce connection with your inner self, a reminder that safety and worth don't have to come from outside in—they start from the inside out.

It's also crucial to extend compassion toward mistakes or perceived setbacks on this journey. Self-trust isn't about perfection; it's about showing up even when you stumble. If you catch yourself falling into old patterns—maybe doubting your worth after a triggering moment—pause. Instead of spiraling into self-criticism, gently ask, "What does this moment want me to learn?" or "How can I be kinder to myself right now?" In doing so, you turn mistakes into lessons and reinforce the idea that you're your own ally, not your harshest judge.

Another element often overlooked is the tone and quality of your inner dialogue. The words you say to yourself become the soundtrack of how you experience self-trust and worth. Are you harsh and demanding, or are you tender and encouraging? Imagine how it feels to hear a close friend talk to you with impatience versus warmth. The person most deserving of that friend's kindness is you. Practicing compassionate self-talk doesn't just buffer heartbreak; it reshapes your emotional landscape toward one that feels safe and nurturing.

Practicing mindfulness can deepen this relationship with yourself even more. When you become aware of your thoughts, emotions, and body sensations without reacting immediately, you create a space to choose how to respond. This space is powerful because it breaks the cycle of automatic doubt, shame, or overthinking. Each pause you take builds trust in your ability to intercept old habits and choose care for yourself instead. Over time, this leads to a more reliable, soothing inner presence— your own safe place.

Something to remember is that rebuilding self-trust and self-worth after a breakup is not a linear process. Some days, you'll feel deeply connected to yourself; other days, that connection may fray. That's okay. The practice isn't about never falling off course; it's about returning to yourself with patience when you do. Acknowledge each step forward as a victory, and allow grace for the inevitable steps backward. Both are part of forging a resilient, authentic self.

As you develop this daily practice, notice how external relationships start to mirror your internal growth. When you trust and value yourself, you'll attract interactions that respect and honor those qualities. Conversely, those that diminish your worth will no longer hold the same power. Cultivating self-trust and self-worth is, in essence, reclaiming your authority over your emotional world—becoming the person you feel safest with, no matter what the past held or what the future may bring.

Ultimately, becoming your own safe place through daily cultivation of self-trust and self-worth demands courage and commitment. It's in these small, seemingly private moments of choosing yourself that you begin to rewrite the story of your breakup—from one of pain and loss to one of empowerment and renewal. The journey forward isn't about avoiding vulnerability but learning to stand strong within it, knowing you have everything it takes to thrive, exactly as you are.

Creating Emotional Security From Within is a vital piece of the puzzle when it comes to becoming your own safe place. After a breakup, it's common to feel like your emotional ground has shifted beneath you, as if the stability you once relied on has disappeared. But building emotional security from within is about reclaiming that foundation and learning how to shelter yourself through life's emotional storms. It means cultivating a sense of safety that doesn't depend on anyone else's presence or validation. This process isn't quick or easy, but it's deeply transformative and necessary for genuine healing and growth.

First, it helps to understand what emotional security really means. It's that inner calm where you know you'll be okay, no matter what feelings arise. You might feel sadness, anger, or loneliness — those are natural reactions — but emotional security gives you the strength to face those feelings without falling apart or running away from them. Imagine sitting with grief without being overwhelmed by it, or acknowledging fear without letting it control your actions. This kind of security nurtures resilience, the kind that helps you rebound stronger after setbacks.

How do you begin to build that foundation? It starts with strengthening your relationship with yourself. The breakup might have left you doubting your worth or questioning your ability to move on. That self-doubt chips away at emotional security, making you feel fragile and vulnerable. To counter that, you need to cultivate self-trust — the deep belief that you can handle whatever comes your way, emotionally and practically. One way to do this is to honor your feelings as valid, no matter how messy or uncomfortable they are. Stop fighting parts of yourself that want to heal in their own time.

Consistently showing up for yourself in small ways is another way to build emotional security. This could be through simple daily rituals, like preparing a meal you love, setting aside moments to breathe deeply, journaling honestly about what you're feeling, or allowing yourself to take breaks without guilt. These may seem like small acts, but they're foundational messages to yourself that say, "You matter, and your emotions are worthy of care." Over time, these repeated actions accumulate, reinforcing a sense of stability internally.

We often look to others to provide reassurance after a breakup because that's what human beings have long done — depend on social connection for safety. But depending exclusively on external factors for emotional security is risky. People's availability can change, and relying on someone else for your emotional safety is like building a house on shifting sand. Instead, imagine building that house on solid rock — your own steady, supportive inner world. Learning to soothe yourself when anxiety spikes or when memories creep in is key. Techniques like mindfulness, grounding exercises, or even practicing compassionate self-talk can create a buffer between harsh feelings and how you respond to them.

Another vital aspect lies in embracing your imperfections and vulnerabilities without shame. It's tempting to want to appear strong, especially in the aftermath of a breakup, but true security arises when you

87

accept your whole self — the cracks along with the smooth surfaces. Vulnerability is the birthplace of emotional strength, not weakness. When you allow yourself to be real, you start to dismantle the walls of isolation and build a genuine connection: with yourself. This honesty quietly tells your nervous system that it's safe to relax, which lowers anxiety and emotional reactivity.

Creating emotional security means setting clear, compassionate boundaries with yourself, too. Recognize what thoughts or behaviors pull you into old patterns of pain or self-criticism and gently steer yourself away. For example, you might notice negative self-talk creeping in after scrolling through your ex's social media. Instead of diving into that abyss, acknowledge the impulse, then refocus your mind on something nourishing. This kind of boundary-building is a profound way of signaling self-respect and care.

It's also important to develop a language for your emotions. Many of us default to saying, "I'm fine" or "I'm okay," even when we're anything but. Learning to label your feelings accurately—whether it's frustration, disappointment, or exhaustion—helps you take control over them. Naming emotions decreases their power to overwhelm you and increases your ability to respond thoughtfully. This practice, often overlooked, strengthens your inner safe place by making your emotional landscape easier to navigate.

Building emotional security from within often requires patience and kindness, especially during moments when healing feels fragile. There will be days when anxiety flares up, and self-doubt sneaks back in. Those days don't erase progress but remind you that creating emotional security is a dynamic process. The key is to gently bring yourself back to presence rather than beating yourself up for perceived setbacks. Consistency beats perfection here; steady, small doses of self-compassion are like bricks laid steadily over time building a fortress that lasts.

Engaging in creative outlets or physical movement can also fortify your emotional security. Activities such as drawing, dancing, or hiking aren't just distractions — they reconnect you with your body and your joy, reminding you that you're more than your heartbreak. These moments reinforce that you're capable of generating pleasure and peace independently. When you tap into that source regularly, you prove to yourself that safety and comfort come from within first, not from reliving old attachments or waiting for someone else's affection.

Finally, remember that creating emotional security involves allowing space for growth. You're not trying to suppress feelings or avoid pain but rather to develop a nurturing environment inside, where healing can happen naturally and authentically. You gradually shift from feeling dependent on external validation to feeling whole on your own terms. This internal shift not only prepares you to move on healthier but also sets a foundation for future relationships, grounded in self-awareness and genuine self-love.

In this journey of becoming your own safe place, emotional security is the cornerstone. It transforms the fear of being alone into a powerful experience of self-reliance. It turns the chaos of heartbreak into the calm of personal strength. By investing in yourself, honoring your emotions, and creating habits that support your well-being, you lay down roots that will carry you through this and every challenge ahead.

From Broken to Boundaried

Healing after a breakup means more than just moving on—it's about discovering how to protect your heart without shutting it down. This is where setting clear boundaries becomes essential, transforming feelings of brokenness into personal strength. Learning to recognize what you'll no longer tolerate—and what you truly deserve—is the foundation for healthier connections in the future. Boundaries aren't walls but guardrails that keep you centered and respected, helping you reclaim your sense of self and rebuild your life on your own terms. It's a shift from vulnerability that leaves you exposed to empowerment that nurtures your worth and guides your choices in love and life.

Recognizing Red Flags and Green Flags Clearly is a crucial step when you're moving from feeling broken to establishing firm boundaries. After the crashing waves of heartbreak have settled, it's time to sharpen your vision—not just for future relationships but for how you view yourself and what you deserve. Recognizing red flags and green flags clearly means tuning in to honest, sometimes uncomfortable truths about your experiences and your needs. It's about reprogramming your instincts to identify not only when something is harmful but also when something feels genuinely nourishing and safe.

For many people, the lines between red and green flags get blurry during and after a difficult relationship. You might catch yourself excusing behavior that once made you uneasy, convincing yourself it's normal or that "love means sacrifice." Others might swing to the opposite extreme, viewing anyone new as a potential threat, assuming everyone will hurt you like the last partner did. Neither perspective serves you well. Clear recognition of red and green flags provides the grounding you need to break this pattern, reestablish your worth, and set non-negotiables that protect your emotional well-being.

Understanding red flags isn't about becoming hypervigilant or paranoid. Instead, it's a compassionate practice in self-awareness and boundary-setting. Red flags are those warning signs in behavior, communication, and emotional dynamics that suggest a relationship might be damaging or toxic. They aren't just about flashy moments of betrayal or disrespect; often, they are subtle, persistent issues. These might include things like dismissiveness of your feelings, inconsistent communication, or disregard for your boundaries. Perhaps the person repeatedly blames you for problems, fails to hold themselves accountable, or pressures you to compromise your values.

Red flags become especially important to recognize because they often escalate if ignored. What starts as small discomforts might evolve into serious emotional harm if not addressed. When you clearly identify these signals, you can avoid falling into cycles of self-blame or denial that keep you stuck longer than necessary. It's a way of honoring your experiences and protecting your growth after your breakup. Remember, the goal isn't to catalog faults but to develop a clear-eyed view of what keeps your heart safe and what risks reopening old wounds.

On the flip side, green flags offer a refreshing sense of safety and possibility. They might not always be as dazzling or dramatic as red flags, but they are steady indicators of a healthy connection. Green flags can include consistent honesty, meaningful respect for your boundaries, empathy in communication, and mutual effort in addressing challenges. They are the signs that someone—not perfect, but healthy—is willing to meet you where you're at and grow alongside you.

Discovering green flags after heartbreak can feel like a hopeful hand reaching out in a dark room. These signs show you that relationships can feel empowering,

HOW TO END A LOVE STORY

not depleting. They remind you what it feels like to be valued and heard without sacrificing your identity. Green flags help reframe your relationship standards from fleeing pain to seeking joy, intimacy, and support. Rebuilding your life with these markers in mind puts you in control—it teaches you to recognize when you're moving toward genuine partnership or retreating into old habits disguised as "love."

It's important to acknowledge that the process of recognizing red and green flags is rarely immediate or straightforward. Emotional wounds can cloud your judgment, and old patterns can be hard to break. That's why this step pairs perfectly with building boundaries. Boundaries act as a scaffolding to reinforce your newfound clarity. When you set clear limits, you give yourself space to pause, reflect, and decide whether someone or something fits into your new framework of what's acceptable versus what's harmful.

Assessing red and green flags demands that you actively practice self-reflection and self-trust. This means checking in with how certain behaviors or words make you feel in your gut, your heart, and your mind. Does a comment leave you uplifted or diminished? Does an interaction inspire collaboration or defensive retreat? The more you listen to yourself without judgment, the more skilled you become at gauging what aligns with your well-being.

The complexity of relationships means red and green flags often coexist. Someone might show respect in certain areas but continuously violate key boundaries. Or maybe your own fears are amplifying red flags beyond their reality. This is why clarity takes time and intention. Journaling your experiences, seeking supportive feedback from trusted friends, or working with a therapist can illuminate patterns you might miss on your own. The goal is not to score people but to identify reliable patterns that inform your choices.

As you move forward, recognize that setting boundaries anchored in your awareness of red and green flags doesn't just apply to romantic relationships—it's a lifelong tool for navigating social connections in every realm. When you're clear about what behaviors drain you or nourish you, you're empowered in conversations, decisions, and even in solitude. That strength forms a protective armor that helps prevent the return of damaging dynamics.

Equally important is allowing yourself grace during this learning process. Sometimes, you'll misread a flag, or your feelings will pull you toward familiarity rather than health. That's part of healing. The key is to keep circling back to the question: Does this make me feel whole or fracturing?

Recognizing red flags and green flags clearly isn't a formula—it's a relationship skill you cultivate with patience, honesty, and self-compassion. The more you practice, the more naturally you'll navigate your future relationships with wisdom and heart. This clarity helps you leave behind stories where you were the one who tolerated harm and begin new chapters where boundaries are honored, and your emotional safety is paramount.

In the journey from broken to boundaried, cultivating this skill is transformative. It's not just about saying no to what hurts but also about saying yes to what nurtures growth and joy. When you can identify red flags and green flags with confidence, you're reclaiming your control and your capacity for love—on your own terms and with yourself leading the way.

Redefining Your Relationship Standards begins as a vital turning point when you move from the painful aftermath of a breakup toward a healthier future. After a relationship ends, especially if it left wounds, it's natural to question your own choices and what went wrong. This is not the time to sink deeper into self-doubt or settle for vague ideals about love. Instead, it's an opportunity to clearly define what you value, both within yourself and in a partner, setting standards that protect your well-being and nurture your growth.

When your heart has been broken, the echo of disappointment often clouds your judgment. You might find yourself second-guessing what you should accept versus what you should never tolerate again. This is exactly why redefining your relationship standards is so critical within the process of rebuilding you. It's the space where you reclaim your voice about what love means to you now, away from the emotional residue of past hurts. Setting new standards isn't about constructing rigid rules or unrealistic expectations; it's about honoring your experience by creating boundaries that reflect your worth.

Consider this step as drawing a line in the sand. Before, you might have tolerated behaviors—like a lack of respect, inconsistent communication, or emotional unavailability—because of hope, fear of being alone, or simply not knowing better. But now, equipped with clarity, you're learning to recognize these patterns as red flags rather than nuances you should overlook. This shift demands courage. It means choosing yourself when it feels easier to settle or smooth things over.

Your relationship standards are essentially a blueprint of what you need to thrive emotionally, mentally, and sometimes even spiritually. Rebuilding after a breakup means taking full responsibility for that blueprint. What values are non-negotiable? What qualities in a partner resonate deeply with your authentic self? What compromises are unhealthy and which are reasonable expressions of give-and-take? These questions anchor your path forward. They prevent you from repeating mistakes rooted in unconscious fears or habits.

Most people confuse high standards with being "too picky," but that's a misconception born from societal pressures and outdated norms. Redefining your standards means being wise, not selective for the sake of perfection. It's about knowing that kindness, consistency, and mutual respect aren't luxuries—they're essentials. When you treat these as baseline requirements, rather than exceptions or bonuses, you shift your entire approach to relationships from reactive to proactive.

It's important to acknowledge that redefining your standards doesn't happen overnight. It's a gradual process of peeling back layers of old programming and rebuilding your inner compass. There will be moments where doubts flicker—wondering if you're asking for too much or if these standards will leave you alone. Facing those doubts transparently is part of boundary work. The clearer you get on what's good for you, the easier it is to say no to what isn't.

One key aspect in this journey is self-awareness. Rebuilding you demands an honest inventory of what relationship patterns pulled you down previously. Maybe you attracted partners who were emotionally unavailable, or maybe you overlooked toxic behaviors because love felt like a rescue mission. By recognizing these unhealthy dynamics, you don't just avoid repeating them—you actively unlearn the beliefs that seduced you into them.

Alongside self-awareness, self-respect plays a huge role here. Redefining your relationship standards is essentially an act of self-love. When you start to demand

97

more for yourself, you communicate loudly and clearly what kind of treatment you expect—and will no longer accept. This isn't about arrogance or perfectionism. It's about protecting your heart as fiercely as you would protect your physical health.

There's a profound freedom in this process, too. To realize that you hold the power and responsibility to decide what healthy love looks like for you—untethered from past heartbreak, family pressures, or cultural stereotypes—is deeply liberating. You no longer need to fit yourself into someone else's definition of "normal" or "good enough." Instead, you craft your own authentic standards that align with your truth right now.

As you navigate these new standards, anticipate some inner resistance. Old fears tend to whisper that setting high boundaries means risking loneliness or further heartbreak. But the truth is the opposite: strong boundaries guard you from painful cycles and attract relationships that genuinely fuel your growth. In fact, embracing this mindset shift rewires your emotional expectations—and opens doors to connections that feel safer and more fulfilling.

Practical ways to start redefining your relationship standards include reflecting on past relationships with fresh eyes—what did you tolerate, and what did you thrive with? Write down specific behaviors or qualities that you want to keep out of your future partnerships. Equally important is identifying what you aspire to give and receive. This exercise creates a clear guide for your future choices and conversations.

Communicating these standards early on in future relationships can feel uncomfortable at first, especially if you've been conditioned to avoid "rocking the boat." But honesty from the outset builds a foundation of trust and respect. If your standards aren't aligned, it's kinder and more empowering to part ways sooner than later. This proactive clarity prevents confusion and heartbreak down the line, reinforcing your commitment to emotional safety.

Redefining your relationship standards also involves embracing flexibility without compromise on core values. Nobody is perfect—and understanding this nuance prevents setting unyielding expectations that nobody could meet. It's about holding a firm core while being open to growth and kindness on both sides. Healthy relationships thrive on mutual respect for boundaries rather than control over every detail.

Equally, this process invites you to nurture self-trust. When you're clear about your standards, you learn to trust your instincts more readily. If something feels off or disrespectful, you honor that feeling swiftly instead of ignoring it. Trusting yourself is foundational to developing resilience against unhealthy dynamics that may try to woo you back into old patterns.

Redefining your relationship standards is not just a line item in your personal development checklist— it's a radical act of rebuilding your identity with integrity. It encourages you to grow not just out of heartbreak, but into a stronger, wiser version of yourself. The standards you set become the framework on which your future love stories will be written—with healthier boundaries, deeper respect, and genuine connection.

When you emerge on the other side, stepping into relationships with clearly defined values and boundaries, you'll notice a shift. Dating becomes less about searching desperately and more about mutual discovery rooted in respect. Arguments feel less about survival and more about understanding. Love becomes less confusing and more affirming. And most importantly, you realign with your own worth, no longer sacrificing peace and happiness for the sake of avoiding solitude.

This moment of redefining is one of the hardest yet most empowering phases in rebuilding you. It's where you officially move from being "broken" to being "boundaried." It's the point at which you position yourself not as a victim of past love but as the architect of future fulfillment. With these newly forged standards, you cultivate relationships that honor your true self— and ultimately, you set the stage to love and be loved in a way that's sustainable, respectful, and joyful.

The Level-Up Season

After the storm of heartbreak begins to calm, it's time to claim this chapter as your Level-Up Season—a phase where you don't just recover, but intentionally rebuild and rise stronger. This period invites you to turn inward and rediscover what lights you up beyond the relationship, setting new goals that reflect your truest self. It's about transformation inside and out: embracing your strengths, addressing vulnerabilities with kindness, and cultivating habits that reinforce your worth on your own terms. Though the journey can feel daunting, this season holds incredible power to shift your narrative from loss to growth, helping you step forward with clarity, confidence, and a renewed sense of purpose that honors how far you've come and where you're destined to go.

Glow-Up: Transformation Inside and Out unfolds as a pivotal step in your journey through "The Level-Up Season," where rebuilding yourself after a breakup means more than just moving forward—it means becoming someone renewed, reshaped, and resilient, both inside and out. This transformation is not about superficial changes or quick fixes; it's a deep realignment of who you are, how you see yourself, and how you intend to step into the next chapter of your life with intention and grace.

When a relationship ends, it shakes the very foundation of your identity. You might feel unmoored, like you've lost a part of yourself that was tied to someone else. But this disorientation is also an opportunity—one to reclaim your narrative and redefine your worth on your own terms. The "glow-up" isn't just about changing your appearance; it's about igniting a spark within that fuels confidence, clarity, and compassion for yourself. You start to see the reflection in the mirror differently—not as a reminder of what you lost, but as a symbol of what you're becoming.

Internally, this transformation begins by addressing the self-talk that follows heartbreak. Those critical voices that tell you you're not enough, or that you'll never find love again, need to be challenged head-on. Rebuilding means replacing doubt with affirmation, rewriting those narratives to ones where you are whole and deserving independent of anyone else's validation. This mental shift forms the essential groundwork for your emotional glow-up. It's about cultivating self-compassion and patience—because healing is anything but linear.

Physically, embracing this transformation can take many forms, and it doesn't have to be grandiose. Some find power in fresh routines—morning stretches that awaken the body, walks that clear the head, or cooking meals that nourish both body and spirit. Others dive into more structured fitness practices, not out of pressure to fit a certain ideal, but to rebuild strength and vitality, letting their bodies remind them they're alive and capable. Even small, consistent acts of self-care—a good skincare routine, prioritizing restful sleep, or simply sitting with a cup of tea in quiet—can be profoundly empowering.

Simultaneously, the glow-up involves shedding what no longer serves you. This might mean detoxing your environment by decluttering physical spaces that hold painful memories or removing digital ghosts from social platforms. It's about creating sacred space for new energies to enter your life and for your fresh sense of self to thrive. You reclaim control this way—not only over your surroundings but over the energy and emotions that you allow inside your inner world.

Another crucial element of this transformation is reconnecting with your passions, interests, and dreams, many of which may have been sidelined during the relationship. The breakup offers a chance to rediscover activities that bring you joy and a sense of purpose— whether that's painting, hiking, writing, or learning a new skill. Doing so shifts your focus from loss toward growth, creating opportunities to meet new people, build new skills, and rebuild your identity on your terms. Your glow-up will be incomplete without this re-engagement with what lights you up.

Relationships often involve compromises and sometimes sacrifices. Take time to consider the parts of yourself that you may have set aside to accommodate another person. The glow-up invites you to reclaim those parts—be it your voice, your ambitions, or your boundaries. This re-centering is among the most radical acts of self-love you can commit to after a breakup. It takes courage to honor yourself fully, but this act sets a new precedent: you become someone who refuses to settle for less than what nourishes your soul.

Transformation also means learning to embrace the messy, imperfect process of healing. There will be days when progress feels invisible or like a step backward. Recognizing that these fluctuations are natural helps you maintain momentum without falling into frustration or despair. Your glow-up isn't a destination but an ongoing journey of becoming, one where patience and persistence gradually reveal a stronger, more authentic you.

Building emotional resilience is part of the inside transformation. Heartbreak teaches us painful lessons about vulnerability, attachment, and loss—but it also deepens our capacity for empathy, self-awareness, and emotional intelligence. As you work through the pain, you develop sharper boundaries and a keener sense of what relationships—and life—should look like moving forward. This internal evolution lays the foundation for healthier connections, including the vital relationship you nurture with yourself.

Don't overlook the power of your social circle during your glow-up. This season is a chance to surround yourself with people who uplift and support your growth. Quality friendships become a mirror reflecting your worth and a safe space for vulnerability and celebration. Cultivating these bonds strengthens your new sense of self, reminding you that while romantic love has ended, love in other forms remains abundant and accessible.

Spiritually or philosophically, your transformation might include revisiting your values and beliefs. Breakups often invite us to ask bigger questions about fulfillment, purpose, and direction. Tuning into your inner compass and prioritizing alignment over convenience can empower you to craft a life that feels meaningful and authentic. This realignment recalibrates your priorities, making room for healthier choices and deeper satisfaction beyond fleeting pleasures.

Lastly, embracing the "outs" during this glow-up matters just as much as nurturing the "ins." How you present yourself to the world can have a profound psychological impact. Changing your hairstyle, updating your wardrobe with pieces that reflect your evolving self, or experimenting with new self-expression can all reinforce the internal work you're doing. These external shifts aren't about conforming to trends or seeking approval—they're about affirming your rebirth and celebrating your journey.

Transformation after heartbreak is never a linear upward climb. Instead, it's a spiral—returning to the same themes from different angles, each time with more wisdom. Some days, your confidence will soar; others, you'll question the path. Allow space for this ebb and flow, knowing it signals deep change rather than failure. By actively participating in your glow-up—cultivating mindset, gratitude, self-care, and passion—you set the stage for a powerful comeback that radiates from within and out, preparing you to step fully into your next chapter with conviction and joy.

Setting Goals, Rediscovering Passions, and Self Growth marks a vital turning point in the journey that follows a breakup. Once the storm of raw emotions begins to settle, it's natural—and necessary—to shift focus toward rebuilding not just a life without your ex, but building a richer, fuller version of yourself. This is the essence of *The Level-Up Season*: a time to set intentional goals, reignite parts of yourself that may have been dormant, and actively prioritize your growth. The heartbreak might feel like an ending, but it also opens the door wide for transformation. Now is your moment to grasp that opportunity.

The process of setting goals after a breakup isn't about rushing forward blindly; it's about thoughtful reflection that cultivates clarity. When a relationship dissolves, many lose sight of their individual dreams and desires because they'd been so intertwined with someone else's vision. Reclaiming those personal ambitions starts with asking direct questions: What do I want my life to look like now? What do I need to feel happy, fulfilled, and secure in my own skin? This introspection isn't always easy. It can dredge up doubts and fears about the future, but it's the kind of uncertainty worth sitting with. From there, you craft goals that aren't about distractions or avoiding pain but about nurturing your authentic self.

Goals after a breakup should embrace both the practical and the soulful. Maybe it's rebuilding your career or diving into a new educational path you'd shelved before. Or perhaps it's learning to set boundaries better or practicing daily self-care rituals. These targets serve as anchors, steadying you as your emotional landscape shifts. Importantly, pick goals that feel achievable yet challenging; this balance fuels momentum without setting you up for burnout or self-criticism. Achievement, even in small increments, can rekindle confidence when self-doubt threatens to take over.

Rediscovering passions is equally pivotal in this season of becoming. During a committed relationship, individual interests sometimes take a back seat, especially if you prioritized shared activities or compromises. Now, it's your time to pull those old loves back into your life or explore entirely new terrain. Whether that means reconnecting with art, writing, music, sports, volunteering, or travel, engaging in what stirs your soul can ignite a profound sense of purpose and joy. Passions provide a creative outlet for processing emotions, unlocking new perspectives, and reminding you of the multidimensional person beyond the breakup.

Often, rediscovering passions awakens a deeper understanding of who you are independent of your past relationship. It reclaims the individuality that heartbreak threatens to blur. This process may involve trial and error—picking up hobbies you haven't touched in years or trying out fresh experiences. Each step helps rebuild your identity piece by piece, allowing something vibrant and new to grow from the soil of loss. The key is approaching this rediscovery with openness; there is no right or wrong way to find what lights you up. The goal isn't mastery but connection—to your inner desires and creative flow.

Self-growth during this time doesn't just happen on its own. It requires deliberate action, reflection, and sometimes seeking support when you need it most. This is the season to cultivate emotional resilience by practicing self-compassion and mindfulness. You learn to treat yourself as you would a trusted friend—gently when you're struggling and cheerfully when you succeed. Growth isn't linear; it's messy and uneven, so developing patience with the process itself becomes an essential skill. Each setback or pang of loneliness offers lessons that shape your emerging self.

Part of self-growth is examining and revising the narratives you tell yourself about who you are and what you deserve. After a breakup, it's common to wrestle with feelings of unworthiness or blame. Challenging those damaging internal scripts and replacing them with affirming, truthful messages can shift your mindset dramatically. Affirmations, therapy, journaling, or conversations with trusted friends can support this reframing. Over time, reshaping your internal dialogue fosters a stronger sense of self that's not contingent on external validation or the remnants of a past relationship.

The experience of setting goals and pursuing passions also reintroduces a vital sense of control. When a breakup happens, much feels out of your hands— emotions, circumstances, other people's choices. Defining what you want to achieve places you firmly back in the driver's seat of your own story. It's empowering to decide where to channel your energy next, whether that's starting a fitness routine, enrolling in classes, or simply committing to daily journaling. This form of agency helps replace feelings of helplessness with purposeful action, reminding you that your life remains yours to shape.

Importantly, the goals you set and the passions you rediscover are never just about distraction or busyness. They're about wholehearted engagement. When your heart is aligned with your pursuits, you tap into a wellspring of motivation and fulfillment that radiates beyond the immediate aftermath of loss. This engagement teaches you how to live fully in your own company and offers a blueprint for how you'll create happiness moving forward, relationship or no relationship. In essence, the work you do here becomes the foundation for a future built on self-possession and joy.

This period also invites you to broaden your understanding of self-growth beyond achievements and hobbies. Growth includes cultivating emotional intelligence—recognizing your feelings without judgment, setting healthy boundaries, and communicating authentically. It means practicing forgiveness toward yourself for past mistakes and giving space for vulnerability, not as weakness but as courageous truth-telling. These inner shifts create fertile ground for lasting change and deeper connections down the line.

While it might feel tempting to focus solely on personal goals during *The Level-Up Season*, remember that this growth naturally flows into how you relate to others in the future. When you know what you want, what fulfills you, and how to nurture yourself, you become more selective and clear about who you welcome into your life. Your bar for connection rises, informed by newfound wisdom and standards rooted in self-respect. This evolution is powerful because it centers on thriving within yourself rather than depending on external attachments to feel whole.

Allow yourself moments to celebrate small victories in this phase, whether that's completing a course, rekindling an old hobby, or simply feeling more centered than the day before. Each positive step is a brick in the path toward rebuilding a resilient, vibrant self. Your journey through heartbreak doesn't have to be marked by loss alone; it can be marked by discovery and hope. Setting goals, rediscovering passions, and committing to self-growth are the compass and map that guide you through those uncharted territories.

Ultimately, this Sub-Section is about reclaiming your story on your terms. The breakup opened a painful chapter, yes, but it also cleared space for you to define what's next—your wants, needs, and dreams outside of anyone else's shadow. Use this phase thoughtfully and with kindness to yourself. Transformation feels gradual, but with each intentional step forward, you rise. You level up.

CHAPTER 4

———✦◇✦———

MOVING FORWARD
WITHOUT SETTLING

Choosing to move forward after a breakup means stepping into a future where you refuse to settle for less than you deserve, even when loneliness or the pressure to be with someone tempts you otherwise. It's about holding onto the lessons learned and the growth achieved, knowing that rushing into a new relationship out of fear or habit only masks unresolved wounds that need time to heal. Instead, focus on carving out space for yourself—one where your worth isn't dependent on another person's approval or presence, but rooted deeply in self-respect and clarity. This phase challenges you to stay patient and intentional, trusting that when you're truly ready, you'll attract connections that match your evolved standards without compromising who you are. Embrace this powerful chapter as a foundation for love built on authenticity, resilience, and the courage to choose yourself first, no matter how tempting it may be to turn back or settle for familiar patterns.

When (And If) You're Ready to Date Again

There's no universal timetable for stepping back into the dating world—only your own readiness signals when that time arrives. It's about feeling grounded in who you are outside of any relationship and recognizing that entering a new connection comes from a place of choice, not escape. When you can honestly say you're not chasing someone to fill a void but rather inviting companionship into your already thriving life, you'll set a foundation for healthier, more authentic interactions. Embracing patience with yourself and honoring your healing process ensures you won't settle for less than what truly nourishes your heart and soul. Remember, dating again isn't about rushing to replace what was lost, but about expanding the possibility of love on your own terms.

Avoiding the Rebound Relationship Trap Stepping back into the dating world after a breakup can feel like standing at the edge of a vast ocean — both thrilling and intimidating. When you're finally ready to open your heart again, it's crucial to move forward without rushing or settling for just anyone who crosses your path. The rebound relationship trap is a common pitfall, but it's one you can navigate with awareness and intention. Understanding why rebounds happen, how to recognize them, and cultivating patience will serve as a reliable compass during this sensitive phase.

Rebounds often stem from a deep need to fill the emotional void left by the ended relationship. It's entirely normal to crave connection and reassurance when you're still healing, but jumping into a new romance too soon can cloud your judgment. Instead of establishing a healthy foundation with someone new, you might find yourself clinging to a relationship that actually distracts you from your own growth and healing. This doesn't mean every new connection is a rebound, but the distinction rests in your emotional availability and readiness rather than timing alone.

The pace of emotional recovery varies wildly from person to person. While some might feel comfortable dating within weeks, others need months or more to regain clarity. A rebound relationship often serves as emotional bandage—offering short-term comfort but posing long-term risks. One key sign of a rebound is if the new relationship seems to exist primarily to erase the pain of the past rather than foster genuine mutual connection. It's important to gently ask yourself whether this new relationship supports your evolving identity or unintentionally postpones your healing process.

Another characteristic of rebounds is how heavily they rely on comparison—either idealizing the new partner as "better" than the ex or framing the ex as a failure in contrast. This kind of narrative may feel empowering initially because it fuels emotional distance from past hurt, but it's rarely rooted in reality. Healthy relationships emerge from acceptance, not from running away from unresolved feelings. If your new connection triggers underlying anxieties or seems to accelerate your emotional recovery unnaturally quickly, it might be another sign to pause and reassess.

You might find yourself desperate to avoid loneliness or seeking external validation after heartbreak—and that's okay. Loneliness is painful, and humans are wired for connection. Yet, it's vital to remember that jumping into a relationship just to avoid being alone can backfire. Instead, embrace solitude as an opportunity to learn about what truly matters to you, free from the influence of a partner's needs or expectations. Solitude isn't emptiness; it's a fertile ground for self-exploration and discovering what you genuinely want moving forward.

One practical step is to give yourself permission to date casually, without the weight of expectation. Casual dating allows you to explore connection without rushing into commitment or assuming that every new person you date has to be "the one." It's a way to practice setting boundaries and clarify what feels healthy for you in this season. Avoid the pressure to label every interaction or jump straight into exclusivity. That space can help you differentiate between excitement born of genuine chemistry and the rush of rebound emotion.

Patience is often underrated in this journey. The idea of waiting can feel frustrating, especially when your heart aches for closeness, but it's one of the kindest gifts you can give yourself post-breakup. Patience isn't about stalling or self-denial; it's about building a solid foundation inside yourself before sharing your life with someone else. This inner work ensures that when you do commit, you do so with clarity, confidence, and emotional availability rather than dependency or fear.

It can also be helpful to lean on your support system during this vulnerable transition. Friends, family, or even a therapist can provide honest feedback about your dating choices and emotional readiness. Sometimes those closest to us can spot rebound patterns before we do because they view us from a steadier emotional vantage point. Listening to outside perspectives doesn't mean you're giving up your agency—it means you're fostering wisdom around your decisions and honoring the well-being you deserve.

Knowing your core values and non-negotiables before dating again sharpens your ability to spot rebound dynamics. When you're clear on qualities that matter deeply—respect, emotional availability, shared goals— it becomes easier to recognize if a new interest aligns with your true self or simply serves as a distraction. This clarity isn't about judgment; it's about honoring your own worth and refusing to settle for a relationship that might be convenient but not conducive to your growth.

Remember, every breakup invites reflection and reinvention. The temptation to numb pain through a new relationship is understandable but ultimately unfulfilling. The strongest, most sustainable love stories blossom from a place of wholeness, not incompleteness. By resisting the rebound relationship trap, you're reclaiming your power and setting the stage for connections built on authenticity and mutual respect.

Finally, consider how your rebound relationship fits within your bigger vision for your life. Is this a partnership that supports your dreams, expands your emotional capacity, and encourages your fullest self? Or is it a quick fix to soothe discomfort? These questions keep you grounded and mindful, preventing you from settling too soon or entangling yourself in patterns that might replicate old wounds.

Moving forward without settling means cultivating self-awareness, emotional honesty, and a patience born from compassion for yourself. Avoiding the rebound relationship trap doesn't mean putting your happiness on hold—it means choosing to heal fully, love wisely, and embrace connection in a way that honors your journey and your future.

Attracting Partners Who Truly Align Moving forward after a breakup isn't just about jumping back into dating; it's about stepping into a space where you're truly ready to welcome someone who complements the growth you've achieved. When the time feels right to open your heart again, inviting relationships that align with your values, goals, and emotional needs can make all the difference between repeating old patterns and experiencing authentic connection.

First, it's essential to recognize that the energy you carry after a breakup shapes the kind of relationships you attract. If you've spent time healing and rediscovering your own worth, you'll naturally draw people who respect your boundaries and recognize your newfound strength. This isn't about setting rigid rules but tuning in to what resonates with the core of who you are now. The key lies in clarity—clarity about what you value, what hurts you no longer, and what you aspire to cultivate in a partnership.

Many people fall back into relationships out of loneliness or a desire to prove they're lovable. While that impulse is deeply human, it often leads to compromises that hamper long-term happiness. Moving forward without settling means resisting the rush to fill a void with someone who doesn't truly fit your evolving identity. Instead, the focus should be on quality over quantity— seeking connection that offers mutual respect, emotional safety, and shared vision for the future.

Understanding your non-negotiables before dating again provides a foundation for attracting aligned partners. These aren't arbitrary lists drawn from fleeting frustrations but thoughtful reflections on what you genuinely need in a connection. Do you value open communication? Are you looking for someone who prioritizes growth as much as you do? What about how they treat themselves and others during challenging times? Articulating these qualities drills down to a deeper truth about your preferences and deal-breakers, creating a blueprint to compare potential partners against without scrimping on your standards.

It's also crucial to remember that alignment doesn't imply perfection or sameness but harmony. You don't have to agree on everything, nor should you suppress parts of yourself to fit someone else's mold. Instead, your goal is to find someone whose core values and life path naturally complement yours—someone who encourages your individuality while inviting collaboration and shared experiences. This kind of connection holds space for growth, sparks joy, and sustains respect even when disagreements arise.

One practical step toward attracting aligned partners is being intentional about where and how you engage with potential matches. Online dating apps, social gatherings, mutual friends—each channel draws different types of people. Consider what environments reflect your interests and values. If you're passionate about art, joining a creative workshop or gallery event might connect you with more compatible individuals than a generic social platform. This approach positions you not only to meet people but also to interact as your authentic self, which is magnetic when it comes naturally.

Before jumping into this, ensure your self-awareness is sharp. What parts of your identity have you reclaimed post-breakup? What patterns are you determined to break free from? The more grounded you feel in your own story, the easier it becomes to spot red flags early and shine a light on green flags. Alignment often manifests in the subtle moments: how someone listens to you, responds to vulnerability, or respects your time. Trusting these instincts over surface-level chemistry protects your heart and nurtures a foundation built on mutual respect.

Patience is a virtue that can't be overstated here. It's tempting to want to connect quickly, especially if loneliness lingers. But rushing into something because you want to be 'done' with singlehood often leads to missed signals or overlooking warning signs. Instead, I encourage embracing the waiting period as an opportunity to deepen self-knowledge and affirm what matters most. This way, when you do attract a partner who truly aligns with your essence, it feels less like luck and more like a natural unfolding of your journey.

Another often overlooked component is cultivating a mindset that invites abundance rather than scarcity. Sometimes, after heartbreak, we convince ourselves that the pool of potential partners is limited or that we'll have to lower our standards to avoid being alone. This scarcity mindset can cloud judgment and promote unhealthy patterns. Instead, view your world as full of possibilities, understanding that the right partners will show up when you're in alignment, not desperation. Practicing gratitude for your own growth and the connection you aspire to will set a magnetic tone that others pick up on effortlessly.

It's also vital to consider compatibility beyond the emotional realm. Shared life goals, communication styles, and even how you handle conflict are foundational to alignment. A partner who supports your ambitions and reflects a similar emotional intelligence level often creates less friction over time. This isn't to say differences should be eradicated but that a respectful balance and willingness to grow together needs to be present. Taking time for honest conversations early on about expectations can save heartache and avoid the trap of settling into a relationship that doesn't meet your needs.

When you attract partners who truly align, the experience feels expansive rather than constraining. There's space to be your full self—the parts you've worked hard to heal and the new layers you're eager to explore. This kind of relationship becomes a platform for mutual transformation, not a crutch for emotional survival. Recognizing this difference is part of the ongoing journey of learning how to love healthily again and staying whole during the process.

So, how do you practically approach dating with alignment in mind after a breakup? Start by setting subtle but firm intentions for the kind of connection you want, rather than jumping blindly into availability. Ask yourself what makes you feel safe and seen, and pay attention to how prospective partners show up in ways large and small. Notice their consistency, enthusiasm, and respect for your boundaries; these are signals that you're moving toward something genuine rather than a fleeting distraction.

The willingness to say no to what doesn't feel right is just as powerful as saying yes to what does. This empowerment comes from the self-trust you build through breaking up honestly with your past and choosing growth over convenience. When your foundation is this solid, you're less likely to settle simply because someone is "there." Instead, you open yourself to a relationship with vitality, hope, and the promise of shared joy, reflecting the inner work you've done.

Finally, keep in mind that attracting aligned partners is often about timing and life phase more than urgency. Sometimes, it's not about finding the right person immediately, but about being the right person first. This subtle shift in perspective transforms dating from a task to check off your list into a meaningful extension of your personal evolution. When it happens, it's a partnership that enhances your journey rather than complicates it.

In the end, moving forward without settling means honoring your past while deliberately crafting a future that respects your truth. It invites you to embrace your worth fully, trust your inner compass, and hold space for love that enriches rather than diminishes you. Attracting partners who truly align is less about perfect compatibility and more about authenticity, mutual respect, and shared growth—a love story written with intention, patience, and courage.

Writing a New Love Story With or Without Someone Else

Moving forward means embracing the possibility of a new love story—whether that includes someone else or simply the love you cultivate for yourself. It's about stepping into a future unburdened by past heartaches, where you decide the narrative instead of letting old wounds dictate your next chapter. Writing this new story isn't about rushing into another relationship or fearing loneliness; it's about recognizing your worth, setting clear intentions, and creating healthy connections rooted in authenticity and respect. Whether you find yourself walking this path solo or alongside another person, the key is to stay whole, centered, and true to who you've become through the healing process. This fresh chapter is less about finding "the one" and more about honoring your growth, knowing that every ending was necessary to make space for what's genuinely right for you.

Manifesting Healthy Love and Connection is a vital step in rewriting your love story, whether that next chapter includes someone else or simply the deeper relationship you build with yourself. After the storm of heartbreak and the necessary work of healing, the heart longs not just to fill the void but to connect in ways that foster growth, joy, and authenticity. Manifesting healthy love isn't about rushing into any relationship, nor is it about settling for less than what aligns with your true worth and values. It's about creating space—internally and externally—for connections that reflect the clarity, boundaries, and compassion you've worked so hard to develop.

Many people mistakenly believe that manifesting love means passively wishing or hoping for it to appear as if by magic. But healthy connection requires clarity of intention paired with deliberate action. You need to understand what love looks like for you beyond the fairy-tale versions and cultural scripts that might have shaped your expectations before. What does a partnership that supports your well-being and growth look like? What qualities do you want to bring to a relationship? What kind of connection would inspire and nurture your sense of self rather than diminish it? Taking time to clarify these questions is foundational in manifesting love that truly honors who you are after everything you've been through.

Begin with the recognition that manifesting love isn't just about finding the right person—it's equally about becoming the person who attracts healthy love. This means deepening your relationship with yourself first, which forms the bedrock of all meaningful connections. When you treat yourself with kindness, speak kindly inwardly, and honor your needs and boundaries, you transmit this energy outward. Healthy love seeks reciprocity, respect, and mutual emotional safety. If you're still navigating unresolved grief or harboring doubts about your worth, those energies inadvertently shape the connections you attract. So, before opening your heart again, give yourself room to build emotional resilience.

To manifest healthy love and connection, it's essential to set firm boundaries around who and what you allow into your life. This comes from rewriting the stories you've told yourself in the past about love and worthiness. For instance, if settling was once a survival mechanism, you now have the power to redefine what settling means for you. Instead of accepting less due to fear or loneliness, healthy boundaries help filter out relationships or interactions that might lead you into old patterns of pain. They also communicate to others—and importantly to yourself—that your emotional space is not negotiable. When boundaries are clear, it becomes easier to recognize both red flags and the green flags of a loving, supportive connection.

Manifestation also demands patience and trust in timing. Love that's rushed often skips critical steps of self-discovery and healing, so it's worth approaching dating or opening up with a grounded mindset. Instead of jumping into relationships out of desperation or a need to fill emptiness, focus on cultivating environments where vulnerability can grow safely. This might mean engaging in communities that align with your values, trying new social spaces, or deepening friendships that encourage honesty and shared growth. Each authentic interaction builds toward the kind of connection that isn't just romantic but fundamentally human—rooted in genuine understanding and mutual care.

It's worth noting here that manifesting healthy love doesn't necessarily mean you'll immediately find "the one." Sometimes, the process teaches you how to love fully and richly without another romantic partner—exploring emotional intimacy and fulfillment on your own terms. This capacity to stay whole and grounded can actually magnetize relationships that are healthier because you're entering them from a place of completeness rather than neediness. Love then becomes a choice, a gift freely given and received, rather than a desperate grab to fill gaps left behind. This mindset shift alone can transform your experience of relationships profoundly.

As you rewrite your love story, be intentional about the images and narratives you carry in your mind. Manifesting healthy love means replacing old heartbreak memories and limiting beliefs with new experiences and affirmations that empower. Visualization exercises, journaling about the qualities you want in a partner, or even creating a "love manifesto" can offer tangible focus points. These practices realign your subconscious with the future you desire, building a sense of hope rooted in self-awareness and strength. It becomes easier to spot when a new relationship vibe aligns or when it's time to walk away even before your heart gets tangled up again.

But manifestation isn't without its challenges. Emotional setbacks, unexpected loneliness, or even fear of vulnerability might pop up. Recognize that these moments aren't signs you're failing but invitations to deepen your self-compassion and commitment to clear, authentic love. The process teaches resilience—not by avoiding pain but by learning how to navigate it without losing yourself. It also invites you to release any notions of scarcity about love. There is an abundant reservoir of connection available when you approach it from a place of respect for yourself and others.

Another essential aspect is tuning into your intuition. Healthy love is not only about shared interests or physical attraction; it's about emotional resonance and alignment at a gut level. That inner voice or feeling can often guide you more accurately than external advice or societal expectations. Give space for this intuition to inform your choices by slowing down and paying attention to how you feel around people. Are you relaxed, energized, seen, and safe? Or do you feel tension, guardedness, or pressure to compromise your truths? Manifesting love involves trusting not only your hopes but your instincts.

It's also helpful to remember that healthy connections grow over time. Manifesting love isn't about instant perfection but about the willingness to engage in the messy, joyful, and sometimes challenging dance of relationship-building. When you approach love with curiosity instead of rigid expectations, you allow the connection to unfold authentically. This flexibility prevents disappointment and cultivates patience with both yourself and others. Healthy love requires ongoing communication, forgiveness, and mutual investment—qualities that can only appear when both people feel safe in their whole selves.

Ultimately, manifesting healthy love and connection after a breakup is about reclaiming your power in the narrative of your heart. You get to decide what love means for you, to honor your growth, and to move forward without settling for less than the respect and joy you deserve. Whether or not a new romantic partner enters your life immediately, your capacity for meaningful connection is expanding every day you nurture your worth and boundaries. This is the foundation on which a graceful, empowered next chapter is written—not just as a response to loss but as a celebration of the love that's ready to bloom in its healthiest form.

Staying Whole While Loving Again is one of the most crucial—and sometimes overlooked—parts of moving on after heartbreak. When you've just closed one chapter, especially one that left you raw and vulnerable, you might feel this strong pull to find someone else, to fill a silence or an ache. But what happens when you don't lose yourself in chasing new love? What does it really mean to stay whole while loving again?

Staying whole is not about putting up walls or shutting yourself off from intimacy. It's about carrying your full self—your strengths, your scars, your dreams— into whatever relationship you choose to step into. Think of it as showing up as the complete, healed version of you rather than a version patched together by loneliness or fear. When you stay whole, you offer love from abundance, not scarcity.

Often, after a breakup, people rush into a new relationship hoping it will heal old wounds or prove that they're still lovable. That's a shortcut that rarely works out. It's important to remember that your worth isn't defined by the presence or absence of a partner. Instead, your relationship with yourself sets the foundation for how any new love will grow. If that foundation feels shaky, the new love story might crumble just as quickly as the last one.

Staying whole means knowing who you are outside of any romantic context. It means nurturing your interests, friendships, and passions. At this stage, the focus should be on reconnecting with yourself, not on trying to define yourself through someone else's eyes. You want the sense of your own identity to be so vivid and clear that when you bring someone else into your life, they're joining a celebration rather than saving a person.

One of the biggest challenges in loving again is resisting the urge to compromise away your boundaries. Setting personal limits isn't just about protecting yourself from harm; it's about honoring what you genuinely need and deserve. A healthy relationship comes from two people who respect their own wholeness—and each other's. If you find yourself negotiating parts of yourself to hold on to a partner, that's a red flag telling you to pause and reflect.

The process of staying whole also means honoring your healing timeline. There's no set schedule for when you should be ready to love again. Sometimes the heart opens sooner than expected; other times, it takes months or years. Either way, rushing the process often leads to emotional backtracking. Let your readiness to love be dictated by internal signals, not outside pressures or cultural expectations.

Another aspect of staying whole while loving again is embracing vulnerability with courage. You don't get to skip the messy parts—opening up to someone, risking misunderstandings, and facing fears of rejection are inevitable steps. But loving whole means showing up with your authentic self, even when you can't control the outcome. Vulnerability becomes a bridge, not a weakness.

It's helpful to look at new relationships as opportunities to practice self-awareness and emotional resilience. Each interaction can be a mirror, reflecting parts of yourself you hadn't noticed before. Instead of clinging to the idea that love fixes everything, approach it as a partnership where both people continuously grow and re-learn how to love graciously.

There's also a delicate balance between holding space for a partner and maintaining your own boundaries. Loving again doesn't mean dissolving into their world completely. Instead, it's about overlapping your lives while maintaining individual identities. Healthy interdependence builds on this balance—the freedom to be who you are and the commitment to share that life with someone else.

Sometimes, staying whole can mean loving without anyone else at all. It might mean writing a new love story with yourself as the central character—filling your life with joy, adventures, and connection on your own terms. This choice is just as powerful and worthy. It sends a message that you don't need to settle or fill a void with another person to feel complete.

When you do decide to open your heart again, it's helpful to check in regularly with yourself—to ask: Am I feeling respected? Am I honoring my boundaries? Am

I still prioritizing my healing and growth? Being honest with these questions prevents you from getting lost in the excitement of a new romance and reminds you of your commitment to staying true to yourself.

It's also useful to remember that staying whole involves forgiving—not just others but also yourself. Maybe your last relationship didn't end the way you hoped. Maybe you made mistakes, or maybe you were blindsided. Forgiveness doesn't mean ignoring the lessons learned or erasing pain. Instead, it's about releasing the grip that past hurts have on your present and future. Only when you've offered yourself that grace can you move forward without carrying emotional baggage into your next love story.

True wholeness requires patience and compassion. You might slip up, fall back into old patterns, or question your strength. That's part of the journey. What matters most is getting back up each time, recommitting to the choice of honoring your self-worth and refusing to settle for anything less than authentic love.

The future of your love story doesn't have to look anything like the past. It can be a new kind of story—one written with the awareness and intentionality of someone who has been through the storm and learned how to dance in the rain. Staying whole while loving again is the foundation for a relationship built not on need, but on genuine connection and mutual respect.

Ultimately, the most empowering decision you can make is to prioritize your wholeness above all. When you do, you not only create the conditions for something truly healthy and joyful to enter your life but also cultivate a sense of peace within yourself. That peace radiates outward, attracting people who honor the fullness of who you are.

Never Going Back

Choosing never to return to a past relationship isn't about stubbornness or fear—it's a courageous act of self-respect and clarity. Once you've decided to move forward without settling, revisiting what's behind you only delays the freedom you deserve and clouds the fresh possibilities ahead. Embracing closure means acknowledging the lessons learned without letting old patterns or what-ifs pull you back into familiar pain. It's about trusting yourself enough to know that growth often requires leaving some doors firmly shut, even when the temptation lingers. By refusing to go back, you're making space for new beginnings that align with your worth and vision for love that truly nourishes you.

Choosing Closure as an Empowered Decision marks a pivotal moment in the journey of *Never Going Back*. It's easy to think of closure as something that just happens one day—like a switch flipping off a painful chapter—but real closure is a choice you make. It's a conscious act of empowerment that sets the foundation for moving forward without carrying the weight of unresolved feelings or doubts. Choosing closure means taking control of your narrative, owning your story, and deciding that the next part of your life is yours to shape.

The decision to seek closure reframes the heartbreak from something that happened *to* you into something you're actively working *through*. You're no longer stuck in the endless loop of "what if" or "maybe someday." Instead, you claim the power to define what the ending looks like and, crucially, what it doesn't look like. Closure isn't about revenge, forcing answers from the other person, or pretending everything was perfect. It's about honoring your own needs for peace and certainty, even when parts of the story remain unsaid.

Imagine standing on the edge of a bridge, looking back at everything you left behind in that relationship—the hopes, the pain, the memories—and making the conscious choice not to jump back but to keep walking forward across it. That's what an empowered decision to choose closure feels like. It's not a passive surrender; it's an active release. Closing that door on the past means you're saying, "I see you. I respect what we had. And I am ready to embrace what's next."

One of the biggest challenges people face in breakup recovery is the magnetic pull toward the familiar, even when it's familiar pain. It's tempting to cling to fragments of the past relationship—the texts, the memories, the moments that once felt like love—because it feels safer than stepping into the unknown alone. Choosing closure as an empowered decision reminds you that safety doesn't lie in returning to old patterns or unfinished conversations; safety comes from building internal resilience. It comes from accepting that your worth isn't tied to revisiting a chapter that no longer serves your growth.

When you decide to pursue closure, you're setting important boundaries. This means no longer allowing yourself to be pulled back into cycles of false hope or confusion. You acknowledge that closure can be messy and imperfect, but it's far better than the endless emotional limbo that can trap many after a breakup. You're giving yourself permission to ask for what you need: clarity, honesty—even if it's difficult—and the freedom to walk away without lingering regrets.

Closure is also about forgiving yourself—sometimes even more than forgiving the other person. It's about accepting that you did your best with what you knew at the time, that mistakes were made by both parties, and that the ending wasn't a failure but a necessary conclusion for your well-being. When you hold space for this kind of self-forgiveness, closure becomes less about a tidy, conclusive closing statement and more about an ongoing commitment to your own emotional health.

Another vital piece of making closure an empowered choice comes from rejecting societal scripts that romanticize the painful "getting back together" trope.

Movies and social media often glamorize rekindling love as the ultimate happy ending, but in real life, that path often leads to repeated heartbreak and unresolved issues. Choosing closure means deciding not to engage in that cycle, no matter how tempting it might be to believe that the magic ingredients for "fixing" things will suddenly appear. Instead, you honor the reality that healing is about respect—respect for yourself and for the parts of the relationship that simply weren't compatible.

Sometimes, closure arrives with honest conversations. Other times, it's the quiet resolve that you don't need any more explanations to move on. Both are valid. The key difference in choosing closure consciously is that you *decide* when you've said what needs to be said or when silence must suffice. You regain your voice or reclaim it if you'd lost it during the relationship, and you decide from a place of clarity—not desperation or unresolved emotion.

It's important to recognize that closure isn't necessarily a neatly wrapped package. Life rarely offers such convenient resolutions. Instead, closure often looks like an ongoing process, unfolding over days, weeks, or months. When you own this, it removes pressure and guilt from the equation. You can be patient with your own emotional timeline while holding firm to the fact that you will not go backwards, even if setbacks occur. Choosing closure becomes your anchor, a steady reminder that no matter how long it takes, you are committed to freedom from the past's chains.

To choose closure is to align yourself with hope, not as a naïve expectation but as an intentional belief in your future's possibilities. It's planting a flag inside your heart that declares you won't settle for less than you deserve moving forward. This belief fuels your motivation to rebuild your life on your terms and to engage with healing as a form of active growth.

When choosing closure, you also fortify your trust in yourself. You prove that your intuition and emotional intelligence are reliable guides. This process teaches you how to listen deeply to your own needs and boundaries, an essential skill that safeguards you against repeating patterns of emotional compromise that don't serve you. Becoming the architect of your own closure empowers you beyond just this breakup; it empowers you in all future relationships and life challenges.

Part of this empowerment is recognizing that closure frees you from the emotional and mental energy tied up in the relationship's unresolved threads. By dismantling that emotional baggage, you create mental space for new joy, new connections, and new dreams. This is how you move forward without settling—not by forcing yourself to leap before you're ready, but by holding firm to the belief that you deserve a full heart, not fragments of it pieced together from the past.

Finally, choosing closure sets the tone for your personal narrative moving forward. Instead of seeing yourself as a victim of lost love or someone stuck in sadness, you set yourself up as a survivor and thriver who reclaimed authority over your emotional life. You own your story's ending and take pride that you're not waiting in limbo but are striding toward fresh starts with clarity and dignity.

In essence, choosing closure as an empowered decision is your declaration: you're done going back. No more second-guessing, no more revisiting old pain, no more settling for less than a future that feels whole and intentional. This choice transforms heartbreak into a profound catalyst for self-discovery, healing, and resilience—an act of courage that rewrites your ending not as a close but as an opening to all that's next.

Trusting the Future and Embracing New Beginnings comes as a natural extension to the resolve found in the section "Never Going Back." After deciding to close one chapter decisively, you stand at a crossroads where the unknown stretches ahead. It's an intimidating space, no doubt—filled with possibilities but also with the weight of uncertainty. Learning to trust the future despite fears and doubts isn't about ignoring the past or pretending heartbreak didn't happen; it's a courageous act of faith in yourself and the life you have yet to create.

The moment you commit to never going back, you are, in a sense, opening a door to fresh starts. This is not just about moving on but about moving forward with intention, not just continuing on autopilot. When a relationship ends, especially one that held deep meaning, the instinct to cling to familiarity can be strong. But growth rarely happens within the comfortable walls of what you already know. It demands stepping into a space where you can reinvent your life, your identity, and your happiness on your own terms.

Trusting the future means learning to befriend uncertainty rather than fearing it. Think about how often, after a loss, your mind races ahead to worst-case scenarios or doubts your own ability to thrive solo. Those voices can be persistent. But embracing new beginnings starts with quieting the inner chorus of fear and replacing it with curiosity. Yes, it comes with vulnerability—that uncomfortable, raw feeling of not knowing what's next— but it's also the soil where resilience and self-discovery grow.

One of the most powerful ways to nurture trust in the future is to anchor yourself in the present moment while holding a vision for what you deserve next. This doesn't mean you need a perfect roadmap of your entire life's trajectory; it means acknowledging that you're worthy of happiness and that your future can and should look different than your past. You don't owe anyone explanations for the life you're choosing now. You can own the narrative of your journey—one that includes healing, growth, and eventually, joy—without looking back or second-guessing those decisions.

It's worth reflecting on how often the stories we tell ourselves about the future are based on fears rather than facts. For instance, you might think, "I'll never find someone like them" or "I'm destined to be alone." These assumptions act like invisible chains. But what if you rewrote those stories with self-compassion and possibility? What if you told yourself, "I'm open to surprises," or "I'm capable of inviting love and connection on my own terms?" The mindset shift may feel subtle, but it creates space for genuine hope to take root.

Embracing a new beginning also calls for patience—both with yourself and with the pacing of life. Healing from a breakup doesn't progress on a linear timeline, and chronic impatience can lead to setbacks like rushing into the wrong relationship or falling back into old patterns just for the sake of comfort. Trusting the future means giving yourself permission to move at a pace that feels right, allowing room for reflection, growth, and self-nurturing.

Another critical piece of trusting the future lies in recognizing your own strength. Ending a relationship and choosing not to return isn't a sign of weakness or failure—it's proof of your courage and self-respect. Every step away from pain is a step toward reclaiming your power. Your future is shaped by how deeply you can honor your boundaries today. Embracing new beginnings means you're saying yes to a life that respects your worth, even if it's not yet fully visible.

Imagine standing on the edge of a cliff, looking out over an expanse of unknown territory. It's both scary and exhilarating, right? But it's in that tension—between fear and excitement—that transformation happens. Trusting the future invites you to lean into that moment, to take a meaningful step forward, even if it's just a small one. It might be reconnecting with an old passion, trying a new hobby, or simply opening yourself up to social interactions again. These actions, however modest, are gestures of hope and faith in what's possible.

It's also important to recognize the role of self-compassion in embracing new beginnings. The path ahead will not always be smooth—you will have days when old grief resurfaces or uncertainties feel heavier. Remind yourself that setbacks aren't failures but part of the process. By treating yourself with kindness in these moments, you reinforce your trust that you can handle whatever comes your way, building emotional resilience essential for cultivating a fulfilling future.

Transitioning out of a significant relationship often means confronting identity shifts. Who are you without the person who once played a central role in your life? Trusting the future involves being curious about this new self instead of fearing loss. It's an invitation to explore what makes you feel alive and aligned. Maybe it's rediscovering your values, redefining your goals, or simply choosing how you want to show up in the world. These aren't trivial tasks—they lay the groundwork for future happiness uninterrupted by unresolved chords of the past.

To truly embrace new beginnings, embracing community and support can also be crucial. Trusting the future doesn't mean walking the road alone. Surround yourself with people who honor your journey and encourage growth. It's a way to reinforce the message that you're not alone in uncertainty and that a network of love and understanding awaits, ready to uplift you as you build your next chapter.

Allow yourself to savor the small victories on this journey forward. Perhaps it's a morning without pain, a reconnecting with an old friend, or a spontaneous moment of joy that reminds you life still holds beauty after loss. These moments serve as evidence that the future is not only survivable but brimful of potential. Holding onto these experiences increases your capacity to trust the unfolding story of your life, inviting you into the grace of new beginnings.

In choosing closure as an empowered decision, you've already taken a significant step—not just away from a past that no longer serves you, but toward a future that holds unknown promise. Let that decision breathe in you. Stand tall in your resolve and trust that life has a way of surprising you when you move forward without settling. The space created by ending one love story is the same space where you get to call forth new chapters—chapters that celebrate your worth, your growth, and the fullness of the life you're building from here on out.

Trust isn't about knowing exactly what will happen. It's about believing in your ability to adapt, to find joy, and to craft a meaningful life, even when the horizon feels hazy. Embracing new beginnings means carrying the wisdom of your past without letting it weigh down your future. It's about opening your heart to optimism tempered with realism, and stepping boldly into the unknown with your spirit intact and your intentions clear. By trusting the future, you're not just surviving heartbreak—you're choosing to thrive beyond it.

CONCLUSION

Ending a romantic relationship is never easy, but it doesn't have to define the rest of your story. As you close this chapter of your life, it's important to remember that healing and growth aren't just possible—they're inevitable when you give yourself the time, patience, and kindness you deserve. This process can feel like standing on the edge of a cliff, uncertain about the fall yet hopeful about what lies beyond. You've taken deliberate steps to understand the pain, navigate the emotional chaos, and rebuild your sense of self. Now, it's time to embrace the freedom that comes from closure and lean into your newfound strength.

It's natural to want quick fixes after heartbreak. Maybe you imagined that the ache would disappear overnight or that reconnecting would somehow ease the wound. But healing is neither linear nor fast. It's messy, unpredictable, and at times, exhausting. What matters most is that you show up for yourself through it all— even on the days when the sadness feels heavy and the future seems unclear. The slow, steady work you've done to process your emotions and redefine your boundaries lays the foundation for a healthier, more authentic life. You are not just surviving; you're emerging.

One of the most empowering lessons here is understanding that your value never depended on the relationship you were in. You are whole right now, in this moment, independently of anyone else's presence or approval. This realization is a game-changer. It shifts the narrative from "I lost someone" to "I am choosing myself." It rewires your mindset from scarcity to abundance—recognizing that love and connection are abundant in many forms, not just romantic. It's a mindset that fosters resilience, allowing you to evolve and attract partnerships that honor the person you've become.

Closure doesn't mean forgetting your past or pretending the relationship didn't matter. Instead, it's about making peace with what was and what didn't work, then gently releasing any lingering blame or what-ifs that hold you captive. Being able to reflect with compassion rather than regret transforms your experience into wisdom. You carry the lessons learned forward, equipped with a clearer sense of what you want—and don't want—from future connections. This clarity is a powerful compass, guiding you toward relationships that match your true self and values.

Remember, it's okay to grieve the ending while also looking forward to the new beginnings ahead. These feelings coexist harmoniously; honoring both creates emotional richness. When you give space to your pain, you also make room for joy and hope. This duality sharpens your emotional intelligence, enabling you to navigate relationships with more authenticity and less fear. Over time, you build resilience that not only protects your heart but allows it to stretch and grow without losing its softness.

Breaking free from the shadows of your past relationship means reclaiming your time, energy, and dreams. It's about rediscovering parts of yourself that may have been tucked away or neglected. You've learned how to nurture yourself from within, creating emotional security that no external circumstance can shake. This level of self-trust is vital—it is the anchor in storms still to come. When your foundation is strong, you can face the unknown with courage instead of doubt.

It's important to acknowledge that moving forward doesn't require rushing into something new or erasing memories. Instead, you decide your pace, your terms, and your readiness. Whether you choose to open yourself to love again or focus solely on self-growth, you are taking control of your narrative. You're rewriting the script from one of loss to one of empowerment. This ownership transforms heartbreak from a setback into a powerful turning point, a catalyst for a richer life experience.

The journey you've been on has equipped you with tools, insights, and a deeper understanding of your emotional landscape. These aren't just for this moment—they're lifelong assets that will serve you whether faced with future challenges or opportunities. Think of this time as the crucible where your new self was forged. You're stepping forward as someone more self-aware, more compassionate, and more committed to honoring your needs unapologetically.

Healing is not about erasing your history; it's about integrating it. The relationship you ended shaped a part of you, and its imprint will always be there, but it doesn't have to dictate your future. Every ending holds the possibility of a beginning, and within that lies your power. You have the capacity to transform sorrow into strength, confusion into clarity, and pain into purpose. When you embrace this truth, you stand ready not just to heal, but to thrive.

As you close this book, take a moment to acknowledge just how far you've come. You've confronted difficult questions and embraced the discomfort needed for reset and renewal. You've done the hard work of untangling emotions and setting intentions that honor your worth. Now, the path ahead is yours to define: with courage, with hope, and with the quiet certainty that you will rise again—whole, healed, and ready to write a new love story, starting with yourself.

The story of healing after a breakup isn't a neat, tidy ending. It's an ongoing process, a continuous unfolding where you grow stronger and wiser with each step.

It's about learning to love yourself fiercely and fully, to trust your instincts, and to move confidently toward a future that reflects your truest desires. Above all, it's about knowing that you are worthy of love, joy, and connection—always have been, and always will be.

APPENDIX

This appendix serves as a practical toolkit designed to support you beyond the pages of this guide, offering a curated collection of resources, exercises, and references to help you navigate each stage of your breakup recovery journey. Whether you're seeking structured tools to manage emotional overwhelm, suggestions for further reading to deepen your understanding, or connections to communities where empathy and growth thrive, you'll find these carefully chosen materials ready to empower you. Healing is rarely linear, but having a reliable arsenal of strategies and support options can make the path clearer and less lonely. Use this section as your personal compass to reclaim strength, find clarity, and remind yourself that rising stronger is entirely within reach.

Tools and Resources for Breakup Recovery

When a relationship ends, it's easy to feel overwhelmed and unsure of where to turn. Recovery isn't just about time passing; it's about having the right tools and resources to help navigate the emotional labyrinth and rebuild your life with intention. This section offers a variety of supportive resources designed to bolster your healing journey, empowering you to move forward with clarity and strength.

One of the most powerful tools available is the practice of journaling. Writing down your thoughts and feelings can be deeply therapeutic. It acts as a mirror reflecting your inner world, helping you recognize patterns and emotions that may otherwise go unnoticed or ignored. Journals don't have to be formal — sometimes a few sentences on what you're feeling in the moment can lead to profound insights. Many people find prompt-based journaling especially helpful because it provides direction during moments of emotional fog.

Alongside journaling, mindfulness and meditation apps have revolutionized how people cope with emotional pain. These resources guide you through breathing exercises, visualization, and grounding techniques. Learning to be present, even when your thoughts want to drag you back into past heartaches or future worries, is a skill worth cultivating. The ability to anchor yourself in the now can dramatically lessen the intensity of grief and anxiety following a breakup.

Therapeutic support, whether in-person or online, is another essential resource. Sometimes heartache runs deeper than self-help alone can reach. Licensed counselors, therapists, or coaches specializing in relationship recovery offer a safe space to unravel confusing feelings and rebuild emotional resilience. Many now offer sliding scale fees or virtual sessions to increase accessibility. Group therapy or support groups can also provide communal healing—knowing you're not alone in your struggle can be both comforting and empowering.

Books and podcasts provide ongoing education and encouragement through both expert advice and personal stories. Reading about heartbreak from different perspectives can normalize your experience and introduce strategies you might not have considered. Podcasts, in particular, offer a sense of companionship, with hosts often walking listeners through the ups and downs of emotional recovery week by week. Make sure to choose recommendations grounded in both empathy and evidence-based approaches.

Digital tools like habit trackers, mood logs, and goal-setting apps help you focus on your personal growth beyond the relationship. They encourage small daily wins, which compound over time into major shifts in self-esteem and confidence. Rebuilding after a breakup isn't just about letting go; it's about stepping into a new version of yourself. Leveraging these resources can make that transition feel less abstract and more achievable.

Creative outlets also serve as valuable resources for healing. Painting, music, dance, or any form of artistic expression provides a way to externalize and process pain when words don't quite capture the depth of your experience. Creativity invites you into a flow state—a mental zone where self-doubt quiets and connection to your inner self reignites. Whether you consider yourself "artsy" or not, exploring different mediums during recovery can surprise you with its transformative power.

Physical wellness resources shouldn't be overlooked either. Exercise, yoga, and nature walks release endorphins that help to combat sadness and stress. Even gentle movement can recalibrate your nervous system, especially when emotional tension feels stuck in your body. Many online platforms now offer trauma-informed fitness and yoga classes tailored to emotional recovery. Prioritizing your body isn't just self-care—it's a foundational step in reconnecting with your own strength.

Social support networks, both formal and informal, play a crucial part in your healing toolkit. Trusted friends and family can offer listening ears and practical help. However, support from those who have walked a similar path—found through dedicated breakup or self-healing communities—can resonate on a different level. These groups often create safe spaces for sharing without judgment, fostering a sense of solidarity that reminds you healing is a shared human experience.

Additionally, setting clear boundaries around digital contact is a modern necessity. Managing social media exposure and digital reminders of your past relationship can dramatically reduce emotional triggers. Numerous apps allow you to mute or block certain accounts temporarily during your recovery phase. This control over your digital environment helps you reclaim mental space and focus on your well-being without constant shocks of nostalgia or hurt.

The power of affirmations and daily reflections is another resource worth incorporating. Affirmations aren't just empty phrases; when crafted with intention, they rewire negative thought patterns that breed self-doubt and despair. Pairing them with your journaling practice or meditations can deepen their impact. This effort to consciously reframe your inner dialogue builds a more compassionate and confident mindset, essential for stepping into your post-breakup life.

For some, spiritual practices or philosophies offer additional layers of support. Whether that means reconnecting with a faith tradition, exploring mindfulness philosophies, or simply finding moments of quiet gratitude, these practices can replenish hope and patience when healing feels slow or uneven. They remind you that you are part of something larger, a perspective that can soften the sting of isolation breakup can sometimes bring.

Last but not least, practical self-care tools such as sleep trackers, nutrition guides, and relaxation techniques contribute quietly but powerfully to emotional recovery. When the body is well-rested and nourished, the mind is better equipped to handle stress and process emotional pain. Attention to these basics can sometimes be overlooked in heartbreak, yet they form the scaffolding upon which psychological healing builds.

In summary, there is no one-size-fits-all answer to getting through a breakup, but the rich variety of tools and resources available today gives you a customizable toolkit. Choose what resonates with you, and don't hesitate to combine practices to craft a support system that truly fits your needs. Remember, recovery is a journey, not a checklist. The most important resource you have is your own willingness to seek support and take small, consistent steps toward reclaiming your sense of self.

With these tools at your side, you're not just surviving the end of a relationship—you're laying the foundation for a future defined by clarity, closure, and a revitalized sense of inner strength.

Recommended Reading and Support Networks

When the dust of a breakup settles, one of the most empowering steps you can take is to seek out resources that provide clarity, comfort, and community. No matter how independent or self-reliant you are, having a trusted go-to list of books, articles, and support groups can add a vital layer of strength to this often-isolating journey. This section is dedicated to pointing you toward well-crafted reading materials and support networks that offer both practical tools and emotional solace, so your path forward feels guided rather than aimless.

Books have a unique way of meeting us where we are emotionally, walking alongside us in ways friends or family sometimes cannot. Whether you're craving practical advice, inspiring stories of transformation, or a deep dive into the psychology behind heartbreak, there's a book out there that will resonate with you. For someone aiming to heal with intention, reading can be a powerful form of self-therapy. It's not just about absorbing information; it's about feeling seen and understood. When a writer articulates what you're experiencing in a page, it can be a relief and a reminder that you are not alone in your pain.

Beyond individual learners, support networks serve as living proof that healing happens in community. You don't have to retreat into silence or suffer in isolation. Many organizations and groups specialize in breakup recovery, emotional well-being, and growth after loss. These networks can be in-person meetings, online forums, or moderated social media spaces where people share stories, offer encouragement, and hold each other accountable in healthy ways. When stuck in a dark place, hearing someone else's breakthrough or simply knowing others show up for one another can spark hope and stamina.

It's important to remember that not every resource suits everyone. Healing is deeply personal—what works profoundly for one person may not connect the same way for another. The key is to approach this list with an open mind, ready to explore new perspectives without pressure. Think of the resources as a buffet of options where you pick what nourishes your heart and mind best.

Exploring recommended reading can deepen your understanding of what breakup recovery really means. Books that weave personal stories with psychological insights can help you reframe your experience and identify patterns that may have influenced your relationship and breakup. They often provide actionable steps you can implement gradually at your own pace. Some may challenge your assumptions, encouraging you to confront emotional blocks, while others remind you to lead with self-compassion and gentleness toward your soul.

Support groups, on the other hand, offer immediacy. Real-time connection with others who are navigating similar emotions lends a different dimension to healing. It reminds us consistently that recovery isn't a lonely battle. Sharing your story out loud, listening to feedback, or simply being in the quiet presence of others' vulnerability cultivates trust and belonging. Trust that leaning on these networks doesn't indicate weakness; it's a sign of courage, acknowledging that moving forward often requires outside support.

For those who want to blend both solitary and communal approaches, some networks also recommend multimedia resources like podcasts or video series inspired by transformative stories. These can fit easily into daily routines or challenging moments where immediate comfort is needed but picking up a book feels overwhelming. They make the healing process accessible and immediate, allowing for connection beyond traditional lines.

Because emotional recovery is ongoing, a recurring practice of revisiting supportive literature and regularly connecting with uplifting communities can maintain momentum during setbacks. Healing is rarely linear. There might be days when you feel strong and self-contained, and others when reaching out feels necessary. Having these resources bookmarked or remembered creates a trusted safety net to fall back upon without shame or hesitation.

While this section doesn't dive into specifics already covered in previous chapters—like how to journal effectively or set boundaries after a breakup—it recognizes those tools as part of the broader healing toolkit that recommended reading and support can reinforce. For example, a book about emotional boundaries might enrich your understanding just when you're trying to enforce no-contact rules. Likewise, a support network could be a place to share your journaling insights and gain new reflections from others who've walked similar paths.

In the digital age, it's essential to be discerning about which resources to trust. Online support can be a double-edged sword—filled both with genuine empathy and, unfortunately, some misguided advice. That's why curated, expert-backed reading lists and moderated support groups hold particular value. They offer a level of credibility and safety that informal channels may lack, giving you the confidence to invest your time and energy wisely.

Recognize too that many of these resources are designed not just for healing but for transformation. They invite you to see beyond the heartbreak and envision a future where you are stronger, wiser, and more self-aware than before. This mindset transforms pain into a catalyst for personal growth and new beginnings rather than a trap of regret or resentment.

Ultimately, incorporating recommended reading and support networks into your breakup recovery journey isn't about finding quick fixes or avoiding your feelings. It's about equipping yourself with knowledge, empathy, tools, and community—things that create a foundation sturdy enough to support your rise from heartbreak toward a renewed sense of self.

In the coming pages, you'll find a carefully selected collection of books and a guide to reputable support networks tailored for anyone ready to put in the work of healing. These suggestions honor different stages of recovery and varying needs, including those looking for emotional empowerment, those seeking practical strategies, and those craving community connection. Use this section as a living resource, returning whenever you need a reminder that help and hope are always within reach.

www.ingramcontent.com/pod-product-compliance
Lightning Source LLC
Chambersburg PA
CBHW032228080426
42735CB00008B/763